"The forest is one big thing; it has people, animals, and plants. There is no point saving the animals if the forest is burned down; there is no point saving the forest if the people and animals who live in it are killed or driven away. The groups trying to save animals cannot win if the people trying to save the forest lose; the people trying to save the Indians cannot win if either of the others lose; the Indians cannot win without the support of these groups; but the groups cannot win without the help of the Indians, who know the forest and the animals and can tell what is happening to them. No one of us is strong enough to win alone; together, we can be strong enough to win."

PAIAKAN, Kayapo leader

THE FATE OF THE FOREST

DEVELOPERS, DESTROYERS AND DEFENDERS OF THE AMAZON

Susanna Hecht and
Alexander Cockburn

$24.95

0 86091 261 2

VERSO
29 West 35th Street, New York, NY 10001-2291

It has always been this way with the mapmakers. From their first scratches on the cave wall to show the migration patterns of the herds, they have traced lines and lived inside them.

Cartographies

MAYA SONENBERG

**WINNER OF THE
1989 DRUE HEINZ
LITERATURE PRIZE
SELECTED BY ROBERT COOVER**

"This is prose of the highest order: tender, provocative, penetratingly intense."
—*Robert Coover*

UNIVERSITY OF PITTSBURGH PRESS

Pittsburgh, PA 15260

$17.95

Edited by Ben Sonnenberg

Associate Editor   Copy Editor
Barbara Jones   Helene Pleasants

Assistant Editor   Copy Assistant
Suzanne Gardinier   Dan Cox

Publisher
Deborah Thomas

GRAND STREET

*is set in Caledonia and printed by
Heritage Printers, Inc., Charlotte, North Carolina.
Drawings on pages 76, 81, 88, 91 and 93 by Monica Incisa.
Drawings on pages 149, 151, 156 and 161 by Edward Sorel.
Cover illustrations by Monica Incisa.
Design by Deborah Thomas.*

Subscriptions $24 a year, $28 foreign. Institutions $28 and $32. Foreign subscriptions (including Canada) should be by International Money Order or otherwise negotiable in U.S. dollars. Single copy price $6, back issues $8. Grand Street is distributed by B. DeBoer, Inc., 113 E. Centre Street, Nutley, N.J. 07110.

Grand Street is published with help from the New York State Council on the Arts, among other generous donors. Grand Street receives no money from the National Endowment for the Arts.

GRAND STREET

Vol. 9, No. 2   *Winter 1990*

In the Spring Issue

JAMES SALTER
A Single Daring Act

PADGETT POWELL
Kansas/Texas

CHARLES MONTEITH
T.S. Eliot in the Office

CHRISTOPHER RICKS
Christina Rossetti

CHRISTOPHER HITCHENS
Burdens and Songs
The Anglo-American Rudyard Kipling
WITH TWO UNPUBLISHED POEMS

QUIET

Rick Rofihe

B est, I like to play things by Ysaÿe, the Belgian violinist and composer. Ysaÿe liked Bach the best. I like Ysaÿe, then Bach.

Bach didn't play violin, but the sonatas he wrote for it are the most beautiful. They say Bach was the bridge between the old and new music; listening to Ysaÿe's music, you know he knew that about Bach.

Even before I touch the bow to the strings, I know that Ysaÿe's music is a bridge between Bach and my violin, and, that when I start to play, the music will be a bridge between my violin and me.

So I play in my funny way—letting my shoulder go as much as I can and tilting my head more than other violinists do. In order to hold the violin as far back as possible, to get its sound as close as I can to my ear.

It's a wonder I don't have an off-center, sideways kind of look—not only from the way I play the violin, but also from moving my head around so much, trying to see what people say. Trying to hear.

But I don't look any the worse for it; I'm good-looking. And blond hair. And blue eyes. And breasts that rest nicely on the rib cage. No, I look good. And I talk O.K. And I play the violin well. I play it very well.

Never in bed, but always when I play the violin, I wear a rubber band in my hair, to hold it behind me, so it doesn't get in the way. And I take off my earrings when I go to bed, and when I play violin, but the rest of the time I leave them in. My mother had my ears pierced when I was just one or two.

I know it's nobody's fault, and that one thing had nothing to do with the other, because it was this way for me since I was born; they just didn't figure it out for a while that with one of my ears I could hardly hear, and with the other, I couldn't, not at all, hear.

Y saÿe had an unusual way of holding the bow—I don't think anyone really knows why he held it that way, just three fingers and a thumb, the little finger off by itself, angled into the air. He could hear O.K.; he didn't hold the violin like I do, way far back. But that's how I started using just three fingers holding the bow, because with my right forearm reaching around so far, keeping my little finger also pressed down seemed to make my wrist tired.

When you play Ysaÿe, you get to play Bach too, because Ysaÿe liked Bach's music so much he'd put little recognizable bits of it into his own.

When I play violin, because I play solo violin, I never play Vivaldi. Vivaldi could play violin, but he wrote for so many instruments in so many ways, he didn't spend much time writing things for just one violin at a time. And Paganini—Paganini was such a good player that it's hard for anyone who's not a virtuoso to really do justice to the greatest things that he wrote. But Ysaÿe wrote his best things specifically with individual violinists in mind; Ysaÿe's things, I could play all night.

Solo violin. Really, solo only. Having someone accompany me on the piano—maybe. But solo violin with no piano is easier for me.

Me in a string quartet? It wouldn't work. Almost as unlikely as me in an orchestra—without a hearing aid, I couldn't really hear the others playing, but with one, it would be a mess. Because a hearing aid isn't very useful to me when there are a lot of sounds around—it brings them all up at me, each with nearly the same loudness; I wouldn't be able to listen to all those sounds and hear myself play.

But at least I've always had the latest in hearing aids, ever since my parents found out I couldn't hear well. I still have the first one in a drawer, the one I started wearing when I was two and a half. So I've always been hearing something either that way, or through special earphones hooked up to tape recorders and record players, things like that. Out in the world though, whether my hearing aid's in or out, if I'm talking to people, the way it's best for me is one person at a time. And it's the same with dancing—I couldn't really enjoy going out to a dance because, with a hearing aid, there are too many sounds, and without one, it's really not possible to hear the music and talk and have fun.

I started a long time ago with boys. Just talking. Maybe kissing. "I'll ask you a question in your ear and you answer in my ear," I'd start. Then, "Do you think I'm prettier than . . . ?" And I'd say the name of the girl I thought was the fifth-prettiest in my class at school. And the boy would always give the same answer: "Yes."

And then I'd ask the question again but with the fourth-prettiest girl's name.

"Yes."

And it would go like that until I said, "So I must be the prettiest."

"Yes." And then he'd get a kiss.

Later, I would get them to hum into my ear while dancing. I would hum in a boy's ear while he hummed in mine. Because it was really the only way that I felt sure of myself when I was moving with somebody else to music. For me, it was the only good way, but for anyone, it's a good way to dance. So without any other music than that, the boy and I would be dancing; the older I got, the more places that led.

My parents weren't hearing-impaired. I'm glad they helped me in the ways that they did, with the doctors and the hearing aids and the special classes and the music lessons, but even though my parents helped me, after a while I didn't much feel like listening to them. As I got older, their voices got fainter and fainter to me, until, like today, I'm as good as deaf to anything they say.

When I got married, they thought I was finally starting to listen to them again, because I was doing something they wanted. Afterward, I would sometimes think that's the way it was, too—but no, really no, it wasn't that way. Anything I'd ever done, I wanted to do. And sometimes the things I was doing—I guess I got pretty wild. But I just wanted to know, to let myself know, I was alive.

So for a while I didn't care about talking, not more than anything else. Then I narrowed my life down and narrowed it down. And as I did, I guess I calmed down. Because I decided what I needed was a man who would talk into my ear. Not just the slow words and short sentences that he might say to me at night, but all kinds of things, before, and after, and the rest of the day, whenever he was around me. Someone who'd bring the world in a little closer. So everything wouldn't seem so remote.

When you can't hear very well, you often miss fine points. The trailing-off of some things, the leading-into of others: their directions, where they are going or come from. You hear something said, and later you may say exactly the same thing, but you say it too directly, or not directly enough. Because when you heard it, you were concentrating so hard on just getting the words you may not have been able to also pick up on just how it was said. I think this might take away from what you say. From what you do.

But even if I'd had perfect hearing, when it came to those things I might have said or done to avoid being alone, I don't know if I would have said or done anything very different.

Besides the violin lessons, I took classes in lip-reading, hand-spelling and sign. Hand and sign, I don't use them too much, since being able to hear a little has kept me mostly in the hearing world. Still, they're good to know. Other ways to talk. And I would feel silly if I came across a deaf person and we couldn't communicate. Lip-reading I do all the time. I really have to. To fill in what I don't hear.

So the violin, lip-reading, hand and sign—but what wasn't easy to learn was the Helen Keller thing. You know, being deaf and blind, at first she could only do the manual alphabet, letter by letter on the hand, but then she learned how to speak to people by touching their lips and faces and feeling the vibrating of sounds in their throats as they spoke; then putting her fingers on her own face, lips and throat until she got everything right.

It wasn't really something that it made sense for me to do, because even if I close my eyes so I won't see someone's lips, if I'm near enough to reach out and feel the sounds in that person's throat, I can hear them anyway. Hear them with one ear, even with my hearing aid out.

I could cover that ear with my other hand so I wouldn't hear anything, and concentrate on the vibrating, but I know from trying that if I do that, it's like being all the way deaf, and I get frightened. Very frightened.

Of course, Helen Keller was using her fingertips to learn how to speak, and I already know how to speak. But she was first learning how, with her fingertips, to listen, and I knew I wouldn't be happy with myself unless I started doing at least that.

I had a few violin teachers. None that were so special and none for too long. I was kind of a wary student; I didn't know if I really wanted to learn or really wanted to not learn. To deliberately not learn, as if there were some responsibility in learning to play. And I was unsure as to why I chose the violin, except that there aren't many instruments where the sound is so close to your ear. As I got more self-confident, though, I could sometimes relax —if you relax and move your feet as you play, it's almost as if you were dancing with someone humming into your ear.

If I play what would sound loud to other people, it sounds just medium-loud to me. Because I'm not used to hearing sounds even that loud. So I play what would be medium-loud to other people, and, for me, that's just what I need. I can hear it; the sound goes right into my ear but to me it doesn't sound medium-loud. To me it sounds quiet.

The minute I get home from work, the very second I get into the apartment, I take my hearing aid out. And I don't put it back in again until I leave the next day. I know, out there in the world, it's a good thing to have; I accept it. But there is, and always has been, for me, like glasses might be to kids who can't see well, something foreign about it. When I was little, I knew I needed to wear it, so I did, but then I refused to wear anything I thought I didn't need. Like bracelets, or necklaces, or rings. I didn't even want a watch. And I wouldn't wear combs, or clips, just a rubber band sometimes to hold back my hair.

But before long, I was wearing all of that, and more.

A woven thing on my ankle. Fine gold chain around my waist. Rings on six fingers.

Now I just wear the earrings, and just one ring. And a rubber band to hold back my hair.

If I had been born all the way deaf, I wonder how would I have found this feeling I sometimes have now. The first time I heard it, it was as if there was another person in the room, telling me what I was feeling. It was a new feeling for me—so new it was almost a new word.

Not that there's not lots of anger in some violin music: there is, but you usually expect it. It's called for, like sweetness. But one time when I was playing something by Ysaÿe, a sweet part, there it was—something beneath the sound, something trying to come through. And when I came to the angry part, it sounded so full that it was as if my violin was playing to me, playing a word and a feeling.

Lately I've been thinking of getting pregnant. Except then I think, what if it's born like me. She might grow up wanting someone who—but I don't think it's too much to ask of someone, to talk into your ear. When he proposed, I told him that's what I wanted most. To have someone who would always do that. To fill me in on all the things I might have missed hearing. To make up for lost time. And to keep me from missing any more things.

"You bet," he said. He said it all moist right into my ear. I heard it and felt it. "You bet." He said it and said it.

So during the ceremony, I thought for sure he would say, "You bet," instead of "I do." I really thought he would. And when he didn't, and it came time to kiss the bride, I thought for sure that was when he was going to do it, to say, "You bet," into my ear. It would have been nice. I don't like to complain, but it would have been nice.

Whenever I play the violin, I take off my earrings. I take off the one from the ear I can hear with, the one closest to the violin, even if it's not a dangly one that might swing against the violin as I play. I don't want anything between me and the violin when I play.

And I take off the other earring, too, even though it's not really in the way. Even if it made any kind of sound, it wouldn't matter. Because it's on the ear that can't hear. But I take it off. To treat it the same as the ear that can hear. To be fair.

Before I get into bed, and before I play the violin, that's when I take off my earrings, but only before I play the violin do I take off my ring. It's not that it would get in my way when I'm playing, and it's not that I take any ring off my other hand, because I wear only one ring now. But I take it off. To be fair. To be fair.

I'm playing two rooms away from him. If there was anything moist about me, it's evaporated into the room, unless maybe there's some sweat trapped between my rib cage and breasts.

Sometimes I edge the bow high up on the fingerboard, like they say Ysaÿe did. And that does give a good sound, a resonating sound.

I hear high-pitched tones better than low-pitched ones. All violinists would agree: you hear and you feel the music you play. But when I say that, it means only the higher notes. The lowest notes, I just feel.

I don't have any earrings on. No earrings, no necklace, no bracelets, no fine gold chain at the waist, and around my ankle, no woven thing.

And it's quiet. In the middle of the night, this apartment can get so quiet, it's like what it must be like to be all the way deaf. And I can get frightened. Very frightened.

Even if I'm here in the middle of the day, because of how little I can hear, I forget that it's not really so quiet. In the day, if I want to remind myself how noisy it actually is, I just have to look out the window.

But in the middle of the night, I know it's quiet. By looking, by the light of the streetlight. On this street at three in the morning, I'm more likely to find moonlight than car lights. Yes, it's quiet; I can see that it is.

I can see that it is, but if I really wanted to be sure, I'd just stop playing, lay down the bow and do the Helen Keller thing. Put my fingertips against the window. Because if there's any sound outside, it vibrates into the glass. If there's any sound out there, my fingertips could tell.

So all I'd have to do now to be sure that it's quiet is to stop playing, lay down my bow and touch my hand to the window. Except I don't want to stop playing.

But it's quiet. You bet. You bet. Violin quiet.

WHAT IS THE WORD

Samuel Beckett

for Joe Chaikin

folly -
folly for to -
for to -
what is the word -
folly from this -
all this -
folly from all this -
given -
folly given all this -
seeing -
folly seeing all this -
this -
what is the word -
this this -
this this here -
all this this here -
folly given all this -
seeing -
folly seeing all this this here -
for to -
what is the word -
see -
glimpse -
seem to glimpse -
need to seem to glimpse -
folly for to need to seem to glimpse -
what -
what is the word -
and where -
folly for to need to seem to glimpse what where -
where -
what is the word -

there -
over there -
away over there -
afar -
afar away over there -
afaint -
afaint afar away over there what -
what -
what is the word -
seeing all this -
all this this -
all this this here -
folly for to see what -
glimpse -
seem to glimpse -
need to seem to glimpse -
afaint afar away over there what -
folly for to need to seem to glimpse afaint afar
    away over there what -
what -
what is the word -

what is the word

ANGELS

Joan London

1.

I slept, I woke, I slept again. In one of my waking times I thought that yes, I had caught the Russian virus. I thought that I had never been to Russia and was therefore extremely vulnerable to a Russian virus. When I woke up again I saw the snow.

I sat up. The roof garden glowed like a Mediterranean beach. Seagulls arrived and scrabbled outside my window. Although they had been coming for weeks now—Maida and Faye threw them bread—I saw them differently. They seemed like a new species come to a new world. Snowbirds. I fell back on my pillow and slept.

The flat was small but the women's voices echoed at me as if they were calling from the end of a long hall. Back from the cold streets their laughter was vast and relieved. I could hear in their voices the breath of snow.

I hoped they wouldn't come in to see me yet. I thought I couldn't stand the onslaught of such energy. But there was more laughter in the kitchen and the crackle of paper—they'd been shopping. Pop! The plug jumped out of the electric jug. A spoon dropped. Then the living-room window scraped open. Silence.

I looked out my window. Sure enough Faye came squeaking across the snow of the roof garden. She sat down on one of the benches and lit a cigarette. I had often watched her scramble over the sill in the living room: now I was witnessing the private end of the ritual. The light fell on her from the flat above, outlined her cap of grey hair. A mug of coffee steamed beside her. She looked like a larger species of snowbird, crouched forward in her puffy silver parka.

Then suddenly she turned towards my window and smiled straight at me. She lifted one hand and wriggled her gloved fingers. I lay still, shocked. How visible was I?

Was there enough reflected light for her to see my face against the pillow, watching her? Or was she smiling on trust, that I was there, awake, and likely to be watching, somewhere in the darkness?

Maida was on the phone, talking to our daughters. I knew it was them by the way she projected her voice, as if to help it across twelve thousand miles. And because she sounded apologetic.

"Oh, what time is it there then? I'm sorry, love, I'd have thought you'd both be up by now." She gave a little defiant laugh.

I could picture Rachel or Jane, yawning by the phone, examining her feet, wondering whether she should wash her hair. The truth was, no time was the right time to ring the girls. Our calls, like those of outgrown lovers, could only be a disappointment, our concern a bore.

"Did you get our photos?" I asked Rachel the last time I phoned.

"Yes," she said. "You both look so *white*. And kind of tense. What are you worried about? I hope you're not worrying about Michael. He's *fine*."

This time none of the children had wanted to come with us. Michael wanted to stay with his teacher, Mrs. Everett. He was very decided about this. Mrs. Everett's son, Chris, is eighteen, four years older than Michael. He is white-blond, with freckled lips, endlessly good-natured, a Christian. He plays cricket with Michael every day. He's a credit to Mrs. Everett, who is also a Christian. They stood together on Mrs. Everett's front steps as we got back into our taxi. They waved, Mrs. Everett and Chris, and Michael watched them waving, his suitcase and cricket bat at his feet. Maida and I turned to the rear window as we drove off, but he was still watching them.

"How's Michael?" I heard Maida saying now. "Have you seen him?"

Maida had tiptoed in to see me. I felt, rather than heard her, as an interruption in the teeming molecules of the air around me. The engine in my head wouldn't allow me to open so much as one eye. This jealous Russian virus!

The night she hit me we had eaten in a restaurant near Trafalgar. It was no more than a tizzied-up hamburger joint, but it was raining, and the process of getting ourselves back to the flat, on one of those shiplike red buses that swished past us, seemed too much to tackle straight away.

But it was not a place to linger. There was a queue. The light, in mock lantern clusters, seemed to shrink back from us, made us feel the hour was late, our table needed. Before we were disposed of, Faye picked up her coffee and waving her little golden box at us, threaded her way to the lower part of the restaurant. This was fenced off with a tasseled rail and a gate marked SMOKING PERMITTED. Maida and I sipped our tea with that seeping of energy we allowed each other. This was when I started to feel it, the tingling all through my limbs as if I was being reminded of something. All my edges started to draw in, and the rhythm of everything beyond me fell slowly out of time.

My eye traveled the room. I saw on the stand by the door our three coats hanging one on top of the other, Faye's parka which kept its human shape, arms sticking out stiffly like a child's drawing, on top of Maida's Burberry, my tweed. Faye had struck up conversation with a fellow smoker, a young man with a shaven head and a shawl around his shoulders. They nodded and laughed, brandishing their forked fingers at one another, and butted out in a shared ashtray.

I studied Maida's gloves lying by her cup, small soft brown leather gloves like paws, bearing the creases of her knuckles, the teardrop of each fingertip. Again and again I measured the distance between the two tables. It seemed to me that behind the tasseled rail, Faye had returned to her own unknowable element: when she joined us at the door she smiled in the kindly, absent way our daughters might when returning home from somebody's arms.

Out on the street again, it had stopped raining and the city's wet glitter made everything tremble with clarity. A middle-aged woman in a raincoat came walking towards us at the bus stop. Swinging her bag, shaking her head, her walk was purposeful as if she was rehearsing something she was going to say. I stepped back for her as she passed.

Thwack! Her handbag struck me square in the stomach.

"That was for *you!*" she shouted, thrusting her face at me, and for a moment I accepted the pure, insistent logic of that glare. Then I clutched my stomach, and it did not seem strange that the street tilted and swung its length of lights above me.

"So sudden," I heard Maida say to the taxi driver. The city tacked with wild accuracy in and out the window beside her.

"That's how she goes," the taxi driver called out over his shoulder. "Laid up thousands—just knocks them down out of the blue."

I didn't try to tell them. It wasn't a sudden arrival, more a recognition, of a presence that had been there all the time. For weeks now, or was it years, I had felt it coursing through my blood, like a drug, something fretful and chill, and now it had started to speak.

London stayed quiet outside my window. There were reports—Maida gave me details from the bedroom door—of burst pipes, derailed trains, roads buried under drifts that were *the deepest, the furthest south . . .* statistics thrived. The snow had taken the country's breath away. And the Russian flu now claimed twelve lives.

Maida and Faye were not daunted. Each morning Maida tiptoed into our bedroom—since my fever she had slept in Faye's room—and dressed in the milky light. I woke to a thief-like rustle, the tiny whirr of a zip. Whispering, they let themselves out the hall door.

Once or twice I got up and walked around the flat. I didn't recognize it. Maps and guides were piled up by the unmade beds in Faye's room. Newspapers were spread around the living-room floor. On the table was a mound of airletters, friendly blue Australian airletters, opened greedily, in the middle, in the wrong way. I stood shivering by the window and watched the birds fight over crusts left for them in the snow.

This was not the first holiday we had spent with Faye. Once when the girls were very small, before Michael, Fay invited us to share a rented beach house with her and Henry Schmitt and their four children. It wasn't a real beach house, it was an abandoned suburban bungalow, with Venetian blinds that no longer opened and an autumn-leaf carpet that smelt sour and dusty like the coat of an old dog. Its front porch faced scrubby sandhills that blocked off the view of the sea. Here Henry sat all day, smoking and reading, sometimes absently pushing the baby's pram back and forward with his big toe. Here, I said, light-hearted, just unpacked, a daughter on my shoulders, we will drink gin and tonic at sunset. This was the first time I had met Henry and Faye.

I came to think of the Schmitt children as a tribe. Their fringes hung in their eyes, they had all inherited Henry's pinched nostrils. They never slept. They rode their battered bikes through the house on long hot afternoons when everyone was supposed to rest. When I held up my hand to stop Luther, the eldest, he stared at me and rode across my foot. Our own little girls became alarming tell-tales.

Even the sea seemed given over to the children. It stretched for miles, warm, knee-deep: no hint of a wave entered that flat bay. I did not know what to do with myself. Each morning I shared the newspaper with Henry across the gritty table. He was a slow reader. While he muttered over the headlines, I started to look through Positions Vacant and Office Space To Let. Later he puddled dishes in grey water in the sink. I dried. There was no question of conversation with Henry unless you felt strong enough for political debate. I paced the house and plotted my future. I stood on the porch and watched Faye and Maida and the children.

All day long they stood by a swing under tuart trees, supervising turns. Faye wore a shirt of Henry's over sagging bathers and a peaked cap pulled low, like a camp leader. Her short legs were snaked with veins. She and Maida slapped sunburn cream on writhing backs, and talked. They talked as they piggy-backed children in convoy across hot sand and prickles. In the kitchen they talked and laughed and waved their knives around while the lino beneath them crunched with sand and spilt cordial.

"What do you two find to talk about?" I knew I sounded disagreeable. I had lain all afternoon in this airless bedroom with a transistor on my stomach, listening to the cricket. Maida was sitting on the end of the bed, quiet again, rubbing cream into her sunburned arms. I thought of how I saw her with Faye, hooting, bent double, as if something had been released in her.

"As a matter of fact, we made a pact today. We promised to take each other's children if anything happened to us."

"Christ! . . . Don't Henry and I have a say in this?"

"The trouble is, Roy, you never think that anything could happen to us."

Someone was wailing in the hall. Maida turned on her way to the door. "I feel relieved," she said.

"A test run," Maida said. She wedged my cap onto my head and wrapped my neck in a red scarf. I had forgotten about the cold in the streets. I had forgotten how to look after myself. I looked in the hall mirror. I saw that my hair, pushed down by the cap, now covered my ears. My square face had become rectangular, my stubbled cheeks now fell into my scarf. I saw a man in an outsize coat, stooping to look at himself with dark, diffident eyes.

"Ready?" Maida said. She and Faye kept saying how glad they were that I was better. Yesterday I had sat in the living room and drunk chicken noodle soup and read the paper. Now the fever's gone you won't look back, they said.

It was true that the pounding had gone quiet. But I couldn't believe that this was for long. All the time I was listening out for its return. But we were booked into a guesthouse in Scotland, a famous guesthouse in the North, with open fires and grouse and deer. We had only got the booking through a cancellation. A little walk in the Square, they said. Try your legs. See the snow. I followed them out of the flat, down the stairs.

The roof garden had not prepared me for it, the vast even-handed whiteness laid across the grubby street, the meticulous quiet. A square black taxi cruised gently by. The whole city had been brought to order.

"Gorgeous, isn't it?" they said. We crossed the road into the Square. Here they stooped and plastered snowballs together in their gloved hands, grinning at each other. They ran, ducking and squealing, and their breath held its shape as it rose towards the great black trees.

I walked a little. The crunch of my footsteps made me shiver: I could scarcely bear the clarity of the air.

It was back. I was not surprised. It seemed natural that it would start up again here, in the snow, as if the same witch had set us sparkling. . . . The glare enclosed me. All around the Square the houses reared up with grinning windows. I heard the women hailing me from a long way off. My eyes sought out the darkness in the bare thickets by the fence, but I could not see the gate.

2.

I put myself in their hands. Our departure was swift, in a freezing dawn: they helped me down the stairs of the flat whispering, as if they were spiriting me away. They stowed me with pillows and blankets into the back seat of the car they had hired. I sat stiffly, like a packed-up corpse in my cap and red scarf, while they ran back to get our bags.

Faye drove, Maida read the map. They seemed very pleased with the car. "If you want to stretch out we can let down the back seat," they said. They said how I would be tucked into my bed in Scotland that night. With feather pillows most likely. And a hot toddy. They laughed.

They found their way to the M1. An uneasy silver light was rising over the rooftops of the suburbs. "Oh, isn't that nice," Maida said. They found the nice in everything, the courteous drivers, the clear signposting, some horses galloping behind a low stone wall . . . I sank lower and lower into my pillows. My head rolled and jolted on my chest. The car was a capsule of throbbing warmth. I thought suddenly of Henry Schmitt, the last time I had seen him, after years. A glimpse, under a banner, passing me in the lunchtime crowd. I saw his round-shouldered lope, his tight fanatic jaw, as he marched, alone, towards the other banners.

I wondered if I would ever return to the world of men again.

[25]

We stopped once, at a roadside café, somewhere far to the north. There were already stars in the afternoon sky. Snow lay piled like surf against the steaming windows. It was a place of clatter and scraping chairs, lone men in suits bent over newspapers, families chewing together in numbed, stricken silence. We might have dreamt it as we entered, out of the arctic air.

We were served by a waitress with skin as fine as powder and an accent we could hardly understand. We sat amongst the hiss of fat and steam, under the neon glare. I watched Faye pace like a sentry with her cigarette outside the door. I could have laid my swirling head down on the plastic cloth, and stayed.

Then I saw a boy at the pinball game in the corner. One pointy shoe rocked over the other as his wrists shook it to life. I must note down the game, I thought, and its highest recorded score, and send a postcard to Michael. Michael likes facts. Before the snow came I had sent him a postcard nearly every day. No answer, of course, no knowing their effect: I sent them off the way I played these games with Michael, without much skill or hope. Then there is room for something else, that sudden lift or flare. He always recognizes it. I look around for him and see it, on his face.

When Michael was nearly three, Maida could take no more. She took the girls out of school and they went on a holiday together. Although there was more work than we could handle in the agency by then, I took a month off to look after Michael. Maida wouldn't leave him with a stranger: she was afraid that would break whatever fragile links he had with us, he would never trust us again.

I told myself it was a holding operation. We had our routines. We steered a careful course around the house, the suburb. There is a playground near us where in summer the slide winks, red hot, and the swing hangs empty in an acre of dead grass. Even now I choose not to drive home that way. Once, in an endless afternoon, I took him to the beach, and while he howled, I gave myself for five minutes to the sea. Sometimes at night, when even the reruns of the *Twilight Zone* had finished, I carried him around the dripping garden, both of us in pajamas. Twisting away from me in his big nappy, he looked over my shoulder at the shadows, his eyes as dark and ringed as a possum's.

I had to leave him, once a week, to go to the office for a couple of hours. Maida said that Faye would mind him for me. He was used to Faye, she said, he would stay with her. He did. She clasped him to her hip and as I drove away I saw that she was picking something off a leaf and he was stretching over her to look.

The same old Faye, I thought. Her own house was like a beach house, a real one, weatherboard with a veranda, lost among peppermint trees. It was no good going to the front door, Maida warned me, it was blocked off, one of the children slept in the hall. I found Faye each time in the back yard, reading. They had made a whole room out there. At the bottom of the back steps, straight onto the grass, they had set chairs and a table and an old velour couch. And all around in the trees, slung over branches, were bathers and towels, a school shirt, pajama pants, a bathmat, flapping peacefully among the leaves.

The last time, just before Maida came back, I was late picking him up. I had a drink with a client and then another with my partner and staff. I found I couldn't always follow what they were saying. My laughter seemed a beat behind the rest. Another drink might help me to catch up, I thought. Faye won't mind. I was careful not to think of Michael. Then I realized I was three hours late. That drive, too fast, to make amends, it was like all the past weeks, years, swerving along the edge, *something is wrong*, Maida said, and then everything was out of line, everything had to be negotiated. To think of Michael was like sending off a silent prayer.

He was asleep on the leaf-shadowed couch. He slept like that, suddenly, deeply, after one of his fits of rage.

"About half an hour after you usually come he started to wail to the skies."

"I'm sorry. I was held up."

"It doesn't matter. He survived. It doesn't matter at all."

She must have smelt the alcohol, and the sweat that slashed my shirt. She must have seen it all. I closed my eyes.

[27]

She put her arms around me.

It was so quiet there, the way a noisy place is quiet when it has been deserted by its usual voices. I saw above her head the strange cloths nesting in the trees. And higher still a fierce whiteness blazed around the edges of the leaves. Everything was strange and yet piercingly familiar, and the stillness held us as we waited there.

Michael stirred. I gathered him up, and kissed her like a wife, and went away.

3.

The North. It was a moving darkness as if the sky kept pace with us. Lights swung in strings and disappeared and sometimes a denser darkness, a huge curved flank, traveled alongside us and then dropped behind. Sometimes trees were revealed, black bare fists held up to us in the headlights. The car warbled and sighed and the rhythm played through my blood until it seemed the whole journey was fired by the energy of fever.

And then silence.

The car was tentlike in weak orange light.

"Where are we?"

"Three or four miles from the guesthouse, we think. But it's snowing so hard Faye can't see the road."

Then later: "It isn't going to stop. We'll have to stay here for the night."

Their voices were calm and soft.

"Lie between us, Roy, for the warmth."

Feeble and clumsy in my thick coat, I eased myself into the bed they had made in the back for the three of us. Side by side we stared at the ceiling.

"Abraham and his Two Wives," Faye said into the darkness.

"If I remember rightly," I said, "wasn't one of Abraham's wives *young?*"

They thought this was very funny.

They seemed cheerful and matter-of-fact. The guesthouse was expecting us. Tomorrow there would be a search party. Or in the light we would see how ridiculously close we were, and would set off walking, lugging our bags across the snowy fields. Thank goodness there are no children with us, they said, hooting a little in the darkness. They would never let us forget this . . . They yawned and snuggled down. It was almost as if this was part of the plan. And all at once I thought of their maps and whispers, their haste, their insistence, dragging me and my Russian flu on and on, right into the arms of the snow . . . they had all conspired against me . . . they had got me where they wanted me . . .

A sound broke out of me that I didn't recognize, the deep rasp of a stranger, talking through me. I felt it scrape against my ribs and throat. My limbs trailed and twitched behind it. Tears ran from my eyes.

They went quiet then. Maida found my cap and settled it on my head. From time to time one of them would wriggle free of our cocoon and switch on the car engine. The heater roared and snow slithered from the gently vibrating roof. Mist ran in rivulets down the windows, like curtains parting, and we could see the dim broken whiteness flocking past.

Something gripped my chest and tightened. I had to reach further for every breath. And as my eyes closed and my fists clenched, I saw it. I saw her face.

Out of this whiteness crawls the Humber, with my mother and father peering out on their separate sides for street numbers, and the boy in the back, bent over something, something new, a pocket knife. It's a Christmas present. It is Christmas Day, circa 1950.

This is a new suburb, War Service, and we have never been here before. The scrubby grey bush is being pushed back block by block into a valley. The houses are all the same, grey-white asbestos, on stilts at the back for the slope. Nothing is growing here yet, and there are drifts of grey-white sand.

"We need your eyes, Roy," my mother says. She is rather anxious about finding the house, rather annoyed. Christmas Day is a family day, she says. There is something about Harry Crewe and Natasha—never "the Crewes"—whose house we are looking for, that has singled them out, left them adrift, free for drinks on Christmas Day.

Then my father spots Harry on his porch, the Humber wheels down a steep driveway and lurches to a stop with the handbrake. My father, responsible for this outing, gets out first. Squinting, clearing our throats, tucking and patting, my family descends on the porch.

There is a lot of hand-shaking. Harry Crewe is the same as ever, when he comes to pick up my father for golf on Saturday afternoons, except he isn't wearing his tartan cap. He's a solid man with a broad forehead and gold-rimmed glasses. His porch is cool, a slab of glossy red concrete. Natasha is handing round a bowl of cherries. Not just a little damp bagful, a token quarter pound to be scattered in amongst the Christmas nuts and raisins, but a great wooden bowl filled to the top. She shakes it and smiles in front of each one of us. "Take, take," she says.

And when I take a little dangling bunch, it is forked over another, so that a whole linked branchful falls into my lap. My mother looks alarmed, but Natasha laughs and leaves the whole bowl beside me. Then she sits down, not next to my mother, but back next to Harry.

And though my knife is beautifully heavy in my pocket, and I am free to wander off now, I opt for the cherries, which, I can see, are going to be unrationed. And for Natasha. One after another I put the cherries in my mouth, and every word that I have heard, but never listened to, about Natasha, comes flying back to me. She is a White Russian. She has had what they call a Terrible War. Harry Crewe met her in Singapore. She is a woman with no children, but there are other husbands, other wives somewhere. Harry Crewe has given up everything. There are two sides to a story. He doesn't come in for a drink after golf any more because Natasha gets lonely. When my father says the name "Natasha," there's a smile in his voice. He says it quickly and easily to include it in his vocabulary, like the brand name of a new, promising car. He is smiling now, receiving a drink from Natasha, and Harry Crewe is smiling, and my mother, they're all smiling because of Natasha.

Natasha isn't young, she isn't as young as her name sounds. She's as old, maybe even older than my mother. She isn't pretty, but in another way she is like the source of everything pretty in the world. She seems uncluttered, as if, wherever she came from, she could not bring much with her, not even a surname. There are no folds or drapes to her outline. Her hair is coarse and dark, parted, close to her head. She has a long olive-skinned face and her long eyes have a bruised darkness about them. When she smiles, looking into your face, her eyes have a secret life to them, close to something extreme, which might be tears.

My mother talks to her slowly and clearly like she does to our ironing lady, who is a New Australian. But Natasha talks back quickly and laughs, and her laugh breaks ragged and violent across the porch.

Like the men I sit there with my hands on my knees and I look out across the sand to the Humber, held back, mid-turn, down the driveway, and far away down the street I hear kids' voices, rising thin as smoke, arguing over their new toys.

They had turned off the car engine. With every cough I sank back further. I saw our car, a tiny speck amongst the whiteness, and the whiteness spread and became a map of a tiny country, and the map spread and became the globe in Michael's room, set to spin so all the countries blurred together, and the tiny speck, of course, had disappeared.

"I'd give anything for a smoke," Faye said.

I couldn't speak. But in between my gasps, I listened for their steadfast breathing. I am glad you are with me, I wanted to say. But as if they had heard me, they pressed closer to me, their heads beside my shoulders, their hands in mine. An arm pillowed my heavy neck, and I felt a wing of precious breath catch across my cheek.

"Isn't this what you've always wanted?" someone whispered. "To die in a woman's arms?"

USAHN

Suzanne Gardinier

All along there have been places where I
have stopped my sentences to hear you
For every word of this blathering figure
four words' worth of attentive silence This
poem is no more mine than the whorls of my
fingerprints the graves of my ancestors
this Usahn in my mouth and no less Here
is the place for you to speak alive or
dead midwifing this city's birth or
leaving the neckwound cord to its purpose
or sitting by or walking the hallway
outside the red room Here is one place
for you to say your piece although since we
began this journey together you have
started and stopped as you pleased put your two
cents in or offered your silence I
offer this now Tell me what I have not
been able to imagine Tell me
the universes parallel to the ones
I know Tell me your ecstatic breakfasts
what food pleases you what gods if any
Tell me your mother and father your sidewalks
and leaves your exiles Tell me what you have
never told anyone hardly told yourself
Tell me I'm leaning forward to listen

WALKING AWAY WITH HERSELF

Carmel Bird

I like the way X writes.

I love reading stories by X.

I have a friend who says if I can get through the afternoon without mentioning the writing of X, he will give me a rare and exotic plant as a reward. Once I had the opportunity of talking to X in the foyer of a theater where he was going to speak about being a writer.

"Oh, X," I said, "you must have had a very Catholic childhood." And X said, "Yes, I did."

X has written one book about his Catholic childhood and one book about his Catholic adolescence. Many Australian writers have written about their Catholic childhoods. Recently some Australian critics have complained about the number of books about Australian Catholic childhoods. "Let us," they have said, "declare a moratorium on the subject of Catholic childhood in the literature of our country."

X said during the talk he gave at the theater that, when he was a boy, people used to carry their missals to Mass. These missals were usually black, sometimes red. They were books just thick enough to fit comfortably into the hand for carrying. You rested the spine of the missal across the palm of your hand, curling your fingers up the front cover of the book, and your thumb across the back. Missals looked like video cassettes. If you hold a video cassette in the way I just said, you will look as if you are carrying a missal to Mass in the Catholic childhood of X.

One of my video cassettes is very special. It is a tape of a television program about a book I wrote. The book is called *Dog Star*, and they showed it on television as it was coming off the press. *Dog Star, Dog Star, Dog Star*, it went across the screen very fast. As I watched it, I wondered what other books by what other writers were coming off presses at the same time in printing houses all over the world. It's the sort of thing I wonder about. I wonder who else was being born when I was being born. I wonder who will be dying when I am dying, who will share my last day with me, and who will I get for neighbors in the graveyard.

One of the neighbors my mother got was a woman called Dulcie Bull. I can't remember the names of the others, but I often think about my mother and Dulcie Bull lying side by side in front of a row of pine trees. I imagine that the Bull part of Dulcie's name came to her by marriage. My mother acquired the name Power with her marriage. The names Dulcie and Laura seem to me to be at odds with the names Bull and Power. If you said, "We have put Dulcie and Laura together out there under the pines," you would call up a soft, sweet image. But if you said, "We are putting Bull and Power under the pine trees," you would get quite another picture. I imagine the notice in the paper when Dulcie became engaged to Mr. Bull. Then I think of turning over the page and reading what is on the reverse side of the paper. It is an item of historical interest:

"Wife-selling was a popular pastime in old Van Diemen's Land. As women were in short supply, a spouse auction always drew a good crowd. Trading was usually by barter, and recorded instances include examples of wives changing hands for 100 sheep, for 50 ewes, and for five pounds cash and a gallon of rum."

Wives could be troublesome, and in 1818 the following notice was published:

Notice. Whereas my wife Jane is again walked away with herself, without any provocation whatsoever, and, I hear, has taken up with a fellow who looks after cattle, this is to give Notice that I will not pay for bite or sup, or for any other thing she may contract on my Account to any man or mortal; and that I am determined to prosecute with the utmost rigour that the Law will admit, any person or persons who may harbour, conceal, or maintain the said Runaway Jane, after the publication of this advertisement.

Returning to Dulcie and Laura who lie side by side in the graveyard—you would wonder if they ever sat next to each other in the tram or stood one behind the other in a queue at the pictures.

From all this you can see I have an interest in how people's lives intersect. I like to think about the different paths that have led two people to the same place. Perhaps my mother and Dulcie Bull met for the first time in the cemetery.

On Friday mornings, fifteen people come to my classroom to discuss fiction writing. They often read aloud the stories they have been writing recently. Sometimes they write about things that happened to them when they were children. Once a woman was reading out a story about her life as a child in Fiji. She was reading about her birthday party. The woman who had been sitting next to her in the class for several weeks turned to her and said, "I was at the party. I was Edna McMillan. I always came to your parties." Another time two women in the class discovered, through their stories, they had both been in the same class of four-year-olds at a convent. They had both learned to obey the little bell that belonged to Sister Mary Anthony. If you were on the slide or the swing and you heard the little bell, you stopped what you were doing and made the sign of the cross.

"I think it would be interesting," I said, "if you were both to write about it. Then we could compare your memories."

"But are you allowed," another student said, "to write about your Catholic childhood in Australia any more? I thought it was a forbidden subject."

So then I started talking about fashions in writing, and in due course I got round to the subject of X. I realized I would never get my rare and exotic plant at the rate I was going.

Most of the people in my fiction-writing classes are women, and when I look at them I think some of them look a bit like my mother. Then I think about whether my mother would have had time to go to fiction-writing classes. Perhaps she would get on the tram, and Dulcie would get on at the next stop, and they would go to the lecture room at the public library, and the wife of the City Librarian would read them a story by Katherine

Mansfield, and they would discuss the story and start to make up stories of their own. Was there time between the washing and the ironing and the cleaning and the cooking and the cleaning and the shopping and the mending and the sewing and the weeding to write stories and go to fiction-writing classes? They would be writing in the days before the moratorium on Catholic childhoods. They could write:

"We had to make the sign of the cross when Sister rang her little bell."

"I placed the coronet of roses on the head of the statue of Mary."

"I carried a basket of rose petals to scatter at her feet."

They could say to Mr. Bull and Mr. Power,

"We haven't time to sweep the paths, bake the scones, rake the leaves, knit the sleeves, watch the pot, dig the plot, toe the line, sew the seam. We have been crafting our stories, developing our characters, exploring our themes, hatching our plots, paring our language, getting our rhythms, setting our scenes and polishing the perfect sentence."

My mother says: "I have a womb of my own in which to conceive my novel. And I have a fertile brain." She writes the novel, and she calls it *Swing and Slide: The Story of an Australian Catholic Childhood*. And she says, "Wouldn't it be good if television had been invented and there was a program about books and they showed *Swing and Slide* coming off the press? I'd tape the program and then I'd have it on video and I'd be able to watch it whenever I liked. It would go *Swing and Slide, Swing and Slide*, as it went swinging and sliding off the press. And Dulcie would write a book called *Runaway Jane* and the same thing would happen. They would show it on television as it came off the press: *Runaway Jane, Runaway Jane, Runaway Jane*. In *Swing and Slide* I have said some of the things I have always wanted to say. I have them here in black and white on the printed page between covers with a shiny spine that says in thick white writing, 'A Book by Me.' People go into bookshops and say, 'We want a copy of *Swing and Slide* by Mother. And also would you happen to have *Runaway Jane* by Dulcie Bull?

I hear it got a very good review in the *New York Review of Books.*'"

You hear people in the foyers of theaters saying:

"I like the way Dulcie Bull writes."

"I love reading stories by Mother."

A BEATIFICATION

Richard Howard

Began with "A Moral Tale Though Gay," as bold
as brass, as good as gold, or gilt along
the edges, entitled (*sic*) *The Young Duke*
—"though what," old Isaac d'Israeli wailed,
"does Ben know of dukes?"

And closed on the golden molars of the Earl
of Beaconsfield gnashing *The Woman in White* away:
"When I want to read a novel, damme, I write one!"
The interval beguiled to great effect
by a Jew d'esprit,

or so he claimed: "I am the empty page
between the Testaments"—proving thereby
that only the road of appearances may lead
to the palace of essence. And indeed his least
superficial trait

was his frivolity, which from the first
sank to a considerable depth. Consider then
Chapter Seven of Book Two, which the old fox
refused to be persuaded that he wrote:
"I never deny,

I never contradict. But I sometimes
forget." The scene forgotten is the one
where George Augustus Frederick, the young duke,
dresses for a party ("persons of great
consideration:

some were noble, most were rich, all had
ancestors") in something of a rush—
"no time was to be unnecessarily lost
in his preparations (and those of both valets)
for his appearance . . ."

Or for the apparition of a god:
the teakwood dressing-box has been unpacked,
and the shrine for his devotions soon arrayed
with rich-cut flagons of every size and shape
adroitly mingled

with china vases, golden instruments
and the ivory and rosewood brushes, sable-tipped,
worthy even of Reynolds's exquisite device. . . .
His Grace was master of the art of dress
and consequently

consummated that paramount enterprise
with the categorical rapidity of one
whose principles are settled. He then gave
orders with the decision of a Wellington—
the battle was pitched

upon a sparkling plane: ". . . Now let me have
the rose-water—before this dries, you fool!
Light over here, I must have evidence
of how the pores will take another dose
of strychnine. There. Stop!"

The young man's taste was for magnificence;
but he was handsome, and a duke. Pardon him.
Possessed of skin whose pellucid ivory
had never evidenced the Season's strain,
His Grace did not fear

the want of relief ostensibly produced
by a white face, white waistcoat, white cravat.
Set in diamonds, a hair-chain was annexed
to a glass reposing in his waistcoat seam—
this the only weight

the young duke ever bore. It *was* a bore,
but indispensable. The work is done.
He stops one moment at the tall pier glass
and shoots a glance that might have read the mind
of Talleyrand:

it will do! He assumes an air that best befits
the occasion—sublime but cordial—and descends
like a deity from Olympus to dinner below,
the banquet of fortunate mortals who await
an undivulged god.

Had young Disraeli learned the discipline
of being shallow enough for a polite public?
And Beaconsfield, old, discovered after all
that he loathed the vainglory he lived for,
dyed for, rouged for still?

Good to read the dreadful pages, warmed
by these two words together: *much admired.*
Upon him was bestowed that rarest gift,
the Grace of self-delighting fantasy.
Beatified? Yes,

who shows we must hallow *ourselves* if we are
to enter paradise. No good wishing to be
saints like Joan of Arc or John of the Cross—
"der alte Jude, das ist der Mann,"
as Bismarck observed,

an Image of the Truth, if but the truth
of vanity on the grandest possible scale:
illusion without deceit, solitude without
loneliness. The young duke's dressing table,
a map of Eden.

AT THE KIRKS'

Mary Gordon

There were four daughters and a son. The girls were called Constance, Monica, Sabena, Brenda: not an unexceptional name among them. The brother was called J.V., as if his abashment over the distinction of his sisters' names made him feel he had no right to anything but initials. To him, in his army uniform, I took my first steps. He was home from Korea and rarely after that.

My mother knew Mrs. Kirk from church. She agreed to look after me for modest payments. At first, my mother thought that her own mother would look after me. But my grandmother didn't look after any of the other grandchildren and was afraid to cause a family rift. Perhaps, too, my grandmother refused to look after me as a way of highlighting and punishing my father's failure to hold a job.

Why did my mother hire Mrs. Kirk? She was a slattern, with missing front teeth and witch hair. Her housedresses were ripped and loose. I am forgetting though that on those rare occasions when she appeared in public—and this, of course, is how my mother would have known her—she put in her bridge and pinned up her hair. She put on a corset and wool dress with a belt. She appeared presentable: she changed, but nothing ever changed about the house. The darkness of her house was in itself a kind of architecture. What could have made a house so dark? Perhaps it was the bushes that grew up, dense, shaped, around the windows. And it was the blackout shades, pulled down in early afternoon. Still, there must have been some place, some part of a room, a corner of a hallway, where light struck, where a yellowish patch, transected by striped shadows, came to rest on a wooden floor. Some moment of a day when the windows were let open that the house must have been not dark. But I do not remember such a place or time.

I remember heavy furniture. I remember a picture above a chair: fat Romantic girl children with long, black wavy

hair, improperly mature, drapery fallen away to show voluptuous pectoral flesh. I remember a long table in the
dining room that reached from one end of the room to
the other, and the word *mahogany*, which Mrs. Kirk
wanted me to know indicated seriousness and expense. I
thought from listening to her that there were only two
kinds of wood: maple and mahogany. Maple was for the
girls' room. It was the wood of youth.

The house faced on to Scranton Avenue, a busy street.
On its right side was a Howard Johnson's, on its left a
harsh, disturbing vacant lot. So they bounded their property by hedges. A slice in one of the hedges became a path
made up of large uneven stones ending at a grape-colored
shingled porch. The flowers in the garden were night
flowers. I remember nothing springlike, nothing vibrant.
Daffodils and tulips cannot have been planted there. I
think of tiger lilies, threatening with open mouths. And
most of all chrysanthemums, which I would pick too short
and ruin, and be scolded for. I wasn't told not to pick the
flowers, but I was never given scissors. There was general
disappointment when I produced my stunted handful,
graceless as damaged children, all distressing heads. The
response suggested that they believed I ought to have done
better. With a sigh, Mrs. Kirk would indicate the trash can
and sweep out, banging the wooden screen door like a
diva. She would return with a bouquet, ascetic yet luxuriant. She would lay it down on the chipped yellow counter.
She would reach below into a cabinet and bring out a
roll of waxed paper. The sound of the tearing waxed paper
thrilled me in my shame. She would twist the paper into
a crescent or funnel shape and slip the flowers in. "Now
that's nice for your mother," she would say.

Sometimes my mother would come to get me; sometimes
it would be my father. My mother would be driving;
my father would arrive on foot. My mother would drive
up the driveway, a pebbled strip on the side of the property that bordered the vacant lot. There was no way I
could tell that she was coming until the second that I
heard her car whirling up pebbles as she drove in.

She didn't like to get out of the car. She honked her

horn. Mrs. Kirk felt the honor of my mother's professional life had rubbed off on her—my mother was a secretary—and so she was glad to bring me to the car. Leaving me, she left each day a report on my behavior. She and my mother were at war against my secret vice, the private experience of sexual pleasure, which I probably discovered out of the drowning boredom of my days with Mrs. Kirk. "She's been very bad at it," Mrs. Kirk would say, or "She's done quite a number of it today." I never remember her saying that I had been good. A sense of badness like a rinse of dirty water covered me on the ride home. My mother was tight-jawed and angry. Only after dinner, when she listened to the radio, when she ironed and drank coffee or iced drinks did she flower again to the mother I had yearned for all day: fragrant, contained, light, compact. The opposite of life at Mrs. Kirk's, the mother in her crisp delicious clothes who adored me.

My father would arrive on foot. With him, there was a signal I could hope for. I could sit on the front porch and hear, as he walked on the sidewalk in front of the house, still hidden by the hedges, the sound of the coins that clinked together in his pocket. Before I would see him, I would hear the sound of change. *Change.* And things would change. I would run down the path to meet him. He would lift me in one arm and carry me, tipped against his body. He carried a brief case in his other hand: he had to hold that as well as me.

In the time I sat waiting for my father, I was a sponge saturated by longing. I was only one quality, one faculty: I yearned. The clinking sound of his arrival was deliverance. Had I been older, or a visionary child like the Fatima children I later prayed to, I could have prostrated myself on the ground, not before my father, but before the universe for containing within itself the possibility of such complete deliverance, such perfect relief. Mrs. Kirk never reported my badness to my father, partly, I think, because she guessed that he wouldn't believe her, partly because he was male, and partly because she couldn't place him in the world. Who was this man who didn't earn the family money, whose work life she had no proof of (there was none) except his carrying a briefcase, who took days off simply to have his daughter near him, simply to be at home with a child?

I'd guessed that Mrs. Kirk didn't respect my father, but one day she made it clear. I said, "My father is very intelligent." She looked surprised. "Your father?" she said. "It's your mother with the brains. Your mother's as smart as a whip."

I knew then that Mrs. Kirk stood for complete misunderstanding of the world. She didn't understand even that my family was built on a fervid schizophrenic dualism in regard to money. My father's job was to be an intellectual. He wrote unpublishable articles full of references to Charles Péguy and the Desert Fathers. But he didn't earn a cent. His role in our financial life was to create debt; it spread around him like a pool of ink. His plans for magazines, for lecture series, required always an initial small outlay of capital. His only resource was my mother. He would lose the fifty, the one hundred dollars she had forwarded and she would swear never again to trust him with a penny. During these periods, he would have to beg her each morning for the money that he needed to get through the day. "I only want my carfare," I would hear him saying and she would shout, "For what? Where are you going that's worth it? If you spent the carfare looking for a job I wouldn't mind. But I won't give you money for another thing that doesn't get you a good job."

I had a surprisingly firm idea of what a good job would entail. It would be in an office, a room so thoroughly well lighted that there no failure would lodge, a place where there would be cigarette smoke, cigar smoke, the sound of voices and of doors opening and shutting. A place that began activity at a certain hour and ceased it at a time equally well determined. My father would put on his hat and leave that dry, visibly lovable world. And take the train. To us. To me. To get me at the Kirks'. It never occurred to me that if he got a "good job," my mother would stay home. Her life was in the world, as mine would be. As his was. As the Kirks', father and mother, was not. And so the notion of "a good job," that desirable entity my father couldn't seem to grasp, didn't have to do in my mind with a change in our manner of living. It was more a visual idea: an area for my father to inhabit, a new way of moving. His inability to take his place in the world of work, so glamorous for my mother and her boss, a lawyer whom she worshipped, didn't cause either my mother or me to suspect my father's superiority. He failed, but he was not inferior: neither of us had trouble holding, simultaneously, these two thoughts in our mind.

I knew that even though it brought him money, Basil Kirk's job did not take up desirable space. He worked nights in the post office. When I saw him, it was only to observe him sluggishly proceeding through the late afternoon that was morning to him, his jaw, underslung like a bulldog's, covered with a stubble that represented to me all that I must keep away from in the world of men. He moved in the kitchen in the same way that the wet wash arrived, a part of domestic life, but unformed and unrecognizable in its historic function. The shirts would eventually be dried, pressed and hung on hangers; Basil would eventually shave, dress and go out to his job, but I would never witness either transformation and my disbelief that either would happen made me recoil from the steaming laundry and from the man who had the name of husband, father, but who slept all day.

Basil's diurnal imbalance was only one more proof to me of the wrongness of the Kirks' life. I put some of this wrongness down to the fact that they were German. Basil wasn't even Catholic, he was Presbyterian, and although Mrs. Kirk's family traced their allegiance to the Church back for centuries, I found it unconvincing. They were neither Irish nor Italian, like the other people in the parish. I had some notion of Germany's *Northernness*, and I had heard contemptuously spoken the name Martin Luther. Martin Luther, who had ruined everything for everyone through pride, through his refusal to have bent the knee. From the pulpit, triumphantly, priests would tell the story of Martin Luther's last words: "It is so difficult to live a Catholic life but so beautiful to die a Catholic death." It didn't occur to me then to doubt the truth of the story: I couldn't have imagined, then, that lies came from the altar, but how can that story have been true? Luther wouldn't have had Catholic sympathizers with him at his deathbed, and the Protestants, knowing he had already turned into an icon, the very people who'd arranged that there should be a death mask, would have kept the story quiet, even if it had occurred.

The time that Mrs. Kirk took care of me began less than five years after the end of the War, yet for me Germany was Luther and not Hitler. In my dreams, men in brown uniforms shaved the heads of naked women who stood only in their high heels in the center of the town to be punished for a crime I had no way of naming. I treasured a story of French war children hoarding, for months, a stick of chewing gum, a single chocolate coin which the oldest would keep in her pocket and allow the younger to touch, with a moistened index finger which they could lick one time each day. But I didn't connect the War, the Nazis, with the Kirks and their Germanness. It was impossible, though, that I not connect them with Luther. For Mrs. Kirk's ancient father, whom I was instructed to call Grandpa Haubrecht, sat all day in the dark house, himself like a dark stone figure, silent until he broke into a German tirade which was explained to me to be about his hatred of Martin Luther.

All day he sat like stone. Except to light his pipe, he was immobile. He wore a brown suit, peppered with little holes like grapeshot made from the sparks that fell out of his pipe. His teeth were broken down like rocks and brownish yellow. He wore brown bootlike shoes, clean but dull, unlike the hard shoes I had seen on men, hard shoes that took a shine. Mrs. Kirk told my mother about his night crimes. My mother was her confidante. He would escape the house at midnight, Mrs. Kirk would tell my mother, wearing only his underwear, which he slept in. (This, to me, was the most shocking detail: what kind of person wouldn't own pajamas?) He would find his way to the Lutheran church where he would shout, in German, speeches about Luther of the purest filth. Luckily, Mrs. Kirk told my mother, the police who came to get him didn't understand German.

It was with Grandpa Haubrecht that I had my first false human relations. Much of my life was made up of false seeming, but the falsity was unconnected to a specific human being. It consisted of my having to pretend I was

[46]

a child. I knew my family was odd, but I was sure of our distinction as a unit; my parents' superiority to other, ordinary parents was clear to me. And in my connection to them, my differentness could be distinction: at least the possibility was there. But on my own in the world, I knew my differentness only as a hindrance. My interests were not appropriate to my state in life. I hated coloring books, sandboxes, games that involved running, chasing, hiding, being safe on base. I thought comic books were ridiculous, except for one, about a buxom model called Katy Keen. And I liked *Nancy* because I was interested in her aunt. I enjoyed watching movies with my parents, the movies they liked, with real, grown-up and beautifully dressed people, not mice and ducks and pigs and farmers chasing each other to no end. I liked lives of the saints and fairy tales with European illustrations. At four, I liked carrying one of my mother's used black leather pocketbooks: the smell of her powder lingered in the inside compartments; she gave me a lace-edged handkerchief and a nearly used-up lipstick to keep inside the bag. Mrs. Kirk hated to see me with it. One day she presented me with a small red plastic child's pocketbook with a hard plastic snowman glued to the front. "I thought it was time you got rid of that black monstrosity," she said. Monstrosity. The word made me unable to love the object for another second. I saw the virtues of the new pocketbook: it was easier to carry and more colorful. The smiling snowman wished me well. I understood that if I carried that child's pocketbook, I could be perceived as an ordinary child. If I could have about me one of the objects that was a sign of ordinary childhood, I could appear to be the thing I had no interest in actually becoming and yet yearned to *seem to be*.

The only kind of child I was interested in being was the child princess of fairy tale. I liked the clothes; my dream was always to be dressed in full, long skirts. The overalls, the limp, thin dresses and dark wool socks I was condemned to wear were a torment. More: they concealed my real nature. I knew who I was. But it appeared to be impossible that I should move in the world in a way that reflected my true (royal) identity. My second choice, therefore, was to appear to be generous, self-sacrificing, kind. In the saints' lives I adored and in the brief, unsatisfactory glimpses I had of childhood moral heroism in movies, a common theme seemed to be struck: the union of the very young and the very old. This seemed to work well for everyone. I was particularly impressed by the misty gaze of observing adults in movies as they stood watching, touched and grateful for the sight. I decided I would cultivate Grandpa Haubrecht. I didn't like him, I was frightened of him, but that was all the better: the conversion for the both of us would be satisfying. Real.

He sat smoking in his hard chair. His eyes were dead; they looked ahead of him at nothing. They were the stone eyes of statues I had seen and feared. I sat down at his feet. He didn't look at me. I kissed his knee. The material of his pants was stiff; the bone beneath it gave no sign of liveliness. He didn't move or respond. I kissed the knee again. Nothing. Silence. Smoking. The gaze into dead air. I was beginning to feel desperate. I was a child; he was an old man: something was supposed to be felt. I learned the bully's desperate timing. I knocked on his knee ten, twelve, fifteen times and kissed again. Nothing. He smoked his pipe. He never looked at me.

I understood that I was not a child.

The Kirk girls weren't girls at all. Their youth was something I had missed, so I could not believe in it. They locked themselves into my vision fully formed, voluptuous, adult as movie stars, American. They had been cleansed of all their parents' mistakes about the world. None of the errors of the house were theirs.

How old were they? I now have no way of knowing. I can place the older two, Constance and Monica, by their public lives. And by their photographs, Constance in her WAVE uniform, Monica in her cap and gown. Mrs. Kirk took care of me for five years; over that time there must have been, for the girls, some process of maturing, of aging, which I could have witnessed. But of course I did not. No child records gradual, incremental change; the Kirk girls were set for me in varying stages of non-childhood, although for most of the time I spent in her house, Sabena must have been a child. Like me. Or like me, pretending.

I knew Constance only in uniform. She was away in Washington. In the WAVES. The WAVES, a name combining natural and military romance. And then one time, she arrived home a fiancée. Her mother and sisters came together in a spasm of unified action. They carried the dining room table out to the garage. They painted trim and vacuumed the upholstery. They made dishes out of foods that before this never had occurred to them: crabmeat, pecans. I was under their feet and I knew well enough to keep out of the way. I was happy to sit on the couch and stare up at the crepe-paper bell suspended from the ceiling. Miraculous. I had seen it on the dining-room table before the table had been taken out to the garage. It had lain inert, in the shape of a boot like Italy, flat, the color of grey cardboard. Then Brenda had shown me how it worked. She moved it on its hinge: it opened and became white: fragile, full, like spring snow on a branch of apple blossom, like the dresses of the princesses of whose company I knew myself to be. Brenda promised me that she would ask her mother to give me the bell to take home when the party was over. So I was content to sit in the dark living room and worship the crepe-paper bell, a sacred object like the rotting hats of the dead cardinals that hung suspended from the ceiling of St. Patrick's. Only better. I would one day own the object of my veneration. One day I would touch it. One day I would cause it to fold on itself and disappear, or to appear from nothing at my bidding. At my will and at my touch.

Or was this bell, and this activity, not for Constance's engagement party, but for Monica's? It is possible that Constance married apart from the family, quietly and militarily, and came home uniformed with her uniformed fiancé (now husband) only to tell the news. I know that at some point she came home with a baby, and I hated that. I understood that the Kirks saw me as inhabiting the same estate as their nephew, an estate apart from them. I wanted, above all, for them to see that I was linked to them in the exacting enterprise of femaleness that took up and exhausted them. I wanted to be one of them. I wanted to be of the party that dressed and undressed not merely for comfort, the party of perfume that smelled not quite fresh, of the butt ends of cosmetics collected in a glass dish on a bureau, of hair taken from hairbrushes and dropped into the toilet, left unflushed along with the extravagantly half-smoked cigarette with lipstick around its tip. The dark party of the female sex.

But now I am only talking about Monica. It was Monica's physical life that drove the family. Not her beauty, it was not that that drove them, and not force, but her appeal. They were devoted to the response she could evoke in men. They served it; they were happy to.

I saw what Monica could do at firsthand once. Two young men came to the door selling subscriptions to magazines. Mrs. Kirk wasn't home; it was Sabena, Brenda, Monica and me. Monica was in charge. She invited the young men in. They sat down in the living room. She brought them iced tea, made with mint that grew by the side of the house, beneath the dripping hose connection. The young men spoke about their magazines. *Reader's Digest*, they said. *Cue. Look. Life.* Monica listened as if she were from a backward country that had never known such things as magazines. She stared absently. She gave nothing out. She was a kind of receptor: she took in their desire. All three of them seemed stupefied. After a while, both the young men asked her to dinner. The smaller one, who had broken out in the sweat (his hair was already thinning) said: "I'll spend all the money I earned today and take you for a steak dinner." The taller, thinner, shyer one said, "It'll only be beans from me, but it'll be from the heart." I didn't know whether he was poorer than the other one, or simply convinced that no amount of effort on his part would make a difference. He was clearly overmastered by his colleague: he carried the sample case and entered the door behind him. I knew I wanted the tall, thin, defeated one to win Monica, but I knew he wouldn't. In the end, it never came to anything, because my father arrived, and in an uncharacteristic assertion of traditional male authority, he drove the two young men from the house. They got up, ashamed as if they had been interrupted in the transgression they had only dreamed of. Monica seemed grateful to my father, and relieved. I didn't know why; I knew that she had made what happened happen.

She was languid, she was indolent, yet she caused things to occur around her. At her suggestion, her mother and sisters began making bandages for the Cancer Guild, then horses out of braided rags for crippled children. When her interest lagged, the activity would stop: the work would be left out for a while; cloth, pins and scissors would be kept ready on the sideboard, then they would one day not be there.

She had dull, greyish carnal eyes and full lips that didn't smile or laugh readily. To the right of her lower lip there was a perfect mole. She wore sweaters and skirts; no clothing she put on her body ever stood out from it: even her garments could not resist her. When I first knew her, she was still wearing a Catholic-school uniform. How frustrating it must have been for the nuns, who had invented such outfits to make a young girl's sexual allure seem to be beside the point, that on Monica the harsh pleats melted into one another and the stiff bodice over the stiffened blouse lay down, softened themselves, made themselves passive victims on Monica's wonderful breasts.

I didn't think that she was beautiful. There was something fetid about her slow movingness; even as I was drawn to it, I didn't want to be. I preferred Brenda, who was blond, quick, edgy, tomboyish. She liked to wear what we then called dungarees, and plaid shirts, and she was generally in a position of service to her mother, her sisters, to my mother, who paid her to clean our house on Saturdays. She even served me: she would carry me piggyback down the stairs; she was the only one in the family who ever stirred herself to find anything that might interest me to do. When she carried me, I noticed that her sweat smelled like chicken noodle soup. I admired my own power of association. I thought that she would make the perfect cowgirl; I cast her in the part of Annie Oakley, one of my heroes at the time. I feared that she would never marry. Perhaps I hoped that she would not.

I would be glad to see Brenda today, but I would run from Sabena. She excelled in finding me in my avid sinning. She would discover me; she would watch me for a few seconds before letting me know that she was there. She would smile horribly. "I'm going to tell my mother. I have no choice," she would say. I would nod miserably, knowing no act of mine could be effectual. It now occurs to me that probably I could have bribed her. She had the perfect nature for a blackmailer. Interested in the crime herself, accurate in her timing, she would never have stopped watching me. But she liked luxuries—Dutch coffee candies, Tangee lipstick she was not allowed, Evening in Paris perfume in small dark blue bottles. I could have turned thief for her, if I'd thought of it. I could have stolen from my father to keep her mouth shut.

Monica became engaged to George who was a Greek, a banker. He was shorter than she by inches; his hair was stuck to his head with horrifying grease. I didn't understand how he had won her; but I knew he did. I had my evidence. I found, stuck behind one of the pillows of the couch, a letter she had written to him. "Dear Darling," it began.

I don't remember what it said after that; those two words told me everything that I needed to know. It was the final proof I needed that I was a creature so different from Monica that I would never have a chance at an experience resembling hers. I knew that you said "dear," or you said "darling." I knew that you did not say both. No feeling I would ever have for any man would cause me to make that error. And I felt that, knowing that, I would not be chosen, for something of what men chose in Monica was that indolence, that failure of alertness that would cause her to yoke two such improper words

At Monica's wedding, I left early with my father. We left before the cake. That was my favorite part of the wedding: getting my father to leave. No one noticed us, or almost no one: Mrs. Kirk saw, but she didn't care enough about either of our presences to mind. I have no memory of Monica the bride or her sisters, the flowerlike attendants. I don't remember food or music. I remember leaving with my father. Down the path through the split in the hedge.

My mother stayed till the end. She brought me home a piece of cake. She told me to put it under my pillow. That way, she said, I'd see in my dreams the face of the man I was meant to marry.

THE HOSTAGE

Eleanor Ross Taylor

They think of me, in their health.

No corridors where shoes whisper.

    (Once I was seven, my tonsils
    somewhere else in the hospital.)

In their dark,
until the blanket gets warm
they think of me.

Sometimes I'm in their dream:
the happy, ravaged fantasy,
without blood and flesh, no

    whether it's going to hurt,
    how long it's going to hurt,
    how long it's going to hurt that much.

They write cards
at the commercials, between
to and fro.
Answerlessness is a fence
in a film war.

They think of me
not in Latin or Arabic;
in the alphabet they know.

They speak of me,
begging recollection,
then sweating out chimera:
my blue eyes, my step, my grin.

They will never beg to see my scar.

THE EIGHTFOLD WAY
A MASQUE IN FIVE TABLEAUX

Thomas M. Disch

FIRST TABLEAU

A funeral parlor. Flowers arranged about a casket. A single red gladiolus fallen to the floor.

Standing before the casket, his back to the audience, looking down at the Corpse, is a man dressed in the peculiar cutaway clothes in which corpses are dressed. As the lights go up, he turns round and we see that his face is identical to that looking up from the casket.

CORPSE

All right, three guesses who I am. I'll almost
Guarantee you've heard of me, assuming
You read the *Times*, and I don't mean just obituaries.
I'm talking Section A, page one, headlines.
Of course it's true, the minute one dies
Identity's less of an issue: who one was,
What one did, what one was paid for doing it.
The best thing about death is that it is a real
Vacation, no work or worries snuck in the luggage,
A ticket to Hawaii, an empty calendar,
A cloudless horizon. Ask any corpse his favorite color
And he will tell you, blue. The problem
With that, from a dramatic point of view
(And I'm as aware as you are that I'm on this stage—
Or page, as the case may be—and cannot otherwise
Than as a figure of fiction communicate with you:
C'est la mort!), the problem with such a Polynesian
Mode of death is that a living audience
Has little incentive to tune in.
The lovelier the weather we report, the more
We wish you were here, the fewer our listeners.
Only bad news sells newspapers, the latest scoop from—

A large mechanical Mouse runs across the stage, spins around, and disappears under the casket.

[55]

CORPSE

[*after a moment's alarm*]
Hell! Now, there's an example of what I mean:
Rats, and rotting in a coffin, and all the other
Gothic traditions connected with death.
It's worse than fraternities and hazings,
A bigger disgrace than Edwin Meese.
Mice! Rats! Maggots and centipedes!
Even for a disembodied spirit like myself
The mind shrinks from such images, but for you
Who are still organic, how dreadful to think
Of lips and eyeballs and other delicate tissues
Becoming carrion. Embalming is supposed
To help: scavengers take one whiff and scurry off
To meats that have been curried with other spices.
Well, whether rats eat it or not, flesh
Will rot, and the thought's disquieting.
Even now, a corpse, I'd rather think of myself
As a statue than as a side of pickled beef.
Though even with stone there's some attrition.
Just this year a new hunk of the Sphinx
Broke off. But even so, for the long haul
Across the millennia, basalt must beat
Formaldehyde, or even aluminum siding.

*The mechanical Mouse re-enters and listens to the
Corpse with a skeptical smile. He has grown to human
size and is dressed in cheery summer clothes. He's carrying a plastic shopping bag supplied with various
props.*

*The Corpse continues to address the audience, un-
aware yet of the Mouse.*

CORPSE

I've yet to tell you who I am, or was.
Want a hint? Think of the word "shrink."
Think of the social sciences. Not anthropology.
Not soc—

MOUSE

[*playfully*]
　　　　　Perhaps religion? Were you
Some great Divine?

CORPSE

　　　　　　　　In fact, I'm not at all
Religious.
[*turns, sees the Mouse, shrieks*]
　　　　　O Jesus, no! O Christ!

MOUSE

I didn't mean to interrupt. Continue:
You were playing guessing games, and threw "shrink"
Out as a clue. Could it be your surname's Fink?

CORPSE

[*offended*]
Could it be *your* first name's Mickey?

MOUSE

Please don't suggest that, even as a jest!
The Disney people can be fearfully litigious.
I would be off this stage and out of print
In minutes, if they suspected I were not
Generically the merest *mus domesticus*.
Besides, have I his voice, his mien, his air
Of innocence, his sweet neoteny?
I more resemble you, or Marilyn Monroe,
Than Mickey Mouse. Now to the business
(We'll say no more of cartoon animals)
Of your afterlife. How would you like to be
Brought back? Animal, mineral, or (re-in)carnation?

CORPSE

I've only just popped off. Why can't I poke
About eternity a while, meet God, enjoy my reward?

MOUSE

Cheese?

[57]

CORPSE
Beg pardon?

MOUSE
                         Some milk in decay?
Let's see: there's Camembert, Muenster,
A rather stiff Brie. And sliced Velveeta.

CORPSE
Even in the afterlife?

MOUSE
                         "On earth as it is
In heaven" works both ways. I've also got
A tolerable zinfandel. The newly dead
Tend to be thirsty.

CORPSE
[as the Mouse uncorks the bottle and lays out a lunch
on top of the casket]
                         Well, I am fond
Of Camembert, and I always did like plays
Where people ate real food on stage
And drank real liquor. Though it's only the beer
You can believe, when the can is popped
And it comes frothing out. Anything else
Is too easily faked. Vodka's obviously water,
But even a bottle that seems to have been corked—
     [The Mouse pops the cork of the wine bottle and pours
     out two glasses.]
Might prove to be grape juice, or just —
     [They toast and drink.]
                         — water
With coloring added. I'm disappointed.

MOUSE
The wine is real enough. It's *you* who've lost
Your sense of taste, and smell, and all the rest.
For all your lifeless tongue could tell
You might have drunk your own exsanguinated blood
And not an '87 Napa Valley zinfandel.

[58]

CORPSE

Heaven, it seems, leaves much to be desired.

MOUSE

Those were the very words of Tantalus.
If you'd enjoy the pleasures you are used to,
You'll have to be reborn. The process can be
Slow as rusting, for first you must be disassembled
To a subatomic state, letting the elements
Of self flake away like paint, until you're
Simplified into a single quintessential quark.
It's taken some Pharaohs until this century
To shrink until they've fit the flesh of housewives
In the suburbs of Phoenix, Arizona.
But I know a quicker way.

CORPSE

                                        To make me a Phoenix

Hausfrau?

MOUSE

                            Or less, or more. You *won't* be
What you were before, that's the only guarantee.
A potted gingko, possibly; a crab, a crane,
A little bitty baby with no brain.
All things are possible in *this* hereafter
Except for grief, or reverence, or laughter.
The microuniverse in which I'll be your cicerone
Exists without respect for human feelings.
Indifference is beauty, and beauty's truth:
That's all you need to know.

CORPSE

                                                If I'm to play

Dante to your Virgil, I'll have to know
A little more than that.

MOUSE

                            Add this then:
Death can be embarrassing. You must undress.
[*responding to the Corpse's gesture of threatened
modesty*]

[59]

Oh, it's not your rotting flesh you must expose.
You must shrug off your name, your history,
Your pride. All you believed must be denied
And all you loathed accepted.

CORPSE

My name, my name . . . It's already gone,
But not the names I used to drop: Johnson,
Jackson, Jacobs, Michaels, Miller, Moore.
I knew them all, and dined with one or two.
I sent them Christmas cards, and signed them
With my name, my name . . . which has evaporated!

MOUSE

For now that's a sufficient sacrifice
To admit you to the first sub-level
Of your disassemblage. It's through that door.

CORPSE

I see no door.

*The coffin at center stage rotates 90 degrees and re-
volves so that the Corpse is standing face to face with
the embalmed body in the coffin.*

SECOND TABLEAU

*The light quivers. The Corpse tentatively places his
hand on the doorknob of the coffin. There is a rum-
bling sound, as of a vault opening. A blackout. A sudden blast of perfume. When the lights come on, the
Corpse and the Mouse have shrunk down to insect
size, so that the entire set behind them is filled with
the petals of the red gladiolus that lay on the floor
beside the casket.*

CORPSE

Now I remember who you are! Sniffles!
Of the comic-book team of Mary-Jane and Sniffles.
When I was little, I would go out behind the house,
Scrunch down by an anthill and pretend to be her,
Reciting her magic rhyme: "Puff, puff, piffles,
Make me just as small as Sniffles," and she would shrink

[60]

To Sniffles' size, this size, mouse size, and off they'd go
Adventuring in a world where any garbage can
Could become a cathedral.

MOUSE

We're mouse-size now, that much is so,
But no, I'm not Sniffles, and if I were,
It would not be very kind of you to blow
My incognito. Copyright, copyright!
Next you'll insist that I am plagiarizing
Fantastic Voyage.

CORPSE

       Right, I remember it!
That's the one about a team of doctors
Who travel in a teeny-tiny submarine
Along the bloodstream of their patient.
Lord, that takes me back: Nineteen-Sixty-Six!
I would have been . . . Now that's gone, too,
Along with every other memory of being young.

MOUSE

And look how much lovelier the world's become
As a result. Without a past specific to yourself
There is no guilt winding up your nerves
Like an alarm clock, no pre-set agenda to say
Now do this, now do that. You are free
To contemplate a flower for an hour at a time.

CORPSE

[*contemplating the vast petals of the set glumly*]
Yes, if I were so inclined. But flowers
Only put me in mind of sickbeds and biers.
If I were a bee, I'd see things differently
No doubt.

MOUSE

    You might become a bee.

CORPSE

Bing Crosby sang a song to that effect
In some movie where he was a priest,

[*61*]

A song about reincarnation.
[*hums melody of "Aren't You Glad You're You?"*]
No, I don't think I'd like to be reborn
A bee.

MOUSE
You're avoiding the issue,
Which is the power that a flower can exercise
Over our imaginations.

CORPSE
An *hour*
Tickling my nose with a rose? I'd die.

MOUSE
With the ghost of a rose. Why don't you try?

*The Mouse reaches into his bag and takes out a baton.
With his back to the audience, he conducts the Weber-
Berlioz "Invitation to the Dance." As the Corpse is
caught up by the music, dancing with increasing energy, the Mouse offers a voice-over narration.*

MOUSE
You are waking from a dream, a young girl
Home from your first ball, and your pretty head
Tinkles and glows like a crystal chandelier!
Once again the remembered waltz whirls
You through space like a satellite of tulle and lace.

*The Corpse, waltzing, plucks one of the petals of the
giant gladiolus and wraps it round himself, capelike,
exposing, as he does so, a door at the flower's center.
The door opens and from it Nijinsky, in his costume as
the Spectre of the Rose, leaps onto the stage to join the
Corpse in his ever more impassioned dance.*

MOUSE
And then— O can your maiden heart sustain
Such joy!—and then—O heavens, can it be?—
It is he! The ghost of the rose you wore at the ball,
Whose breath is a breeze freighted with fragrances

Of Chanel! of Guerlaine! of Cacharel and Giorgio Armani!
Whose touch is the caress of thousand-dollar bills
Drifting like soot from the chimneys of Paradise.
He whispers to you, he begs to repose on your breast
As on the tomb incised with his name—Nijinsky!

*The naming of the Spectre should coincide with the
high point of the music and with the very quick sub-
stitution of the actor playing the Corpse—wrapped in
the gladiolus petal, whirling into the wings and quickly
back again—by his female counterpart, who is dressed,
like Nijinsky, in the costume traditionally worn by bal-
lerinas in this role. Gladys (as the Corpse's female
counterpart will be called) and Nijinsky perform again,
with great artistry, a passage of their* pas de deux *that
had been less ably executed when the Corpse had been
dancing with Nijinsky.*

*As the music comes to an end, Nijinsky sweeps up
Gladys and bears her off through the gladiolus's door.*

THIRD TABLEAU

*The set represents a part of a complex protein molecule
that extends beyond the stage in all directions. It is
formed of aluminum rods, inflated beachballs, neon
lights, steel girders, and panels of Mylar. From time
to time elements within the protein molecule shift position or vibrate. A variety of humming sounds swells
and ebbs in conjunction with a barely perceptible
strobbing of the light. Gladys and Nijinsky are seated
on the molecule, eating yogurt from paper cups.*

GLADYS

I have this image of myself on a golden throne
Surrounded by a multitude of worshipers,
But whether they're worshiping me or I'm only
A sort of high priestess I can't be sure.
It isn't even clear that I'm a woman, I might be a man.
Perhaps one of the Pharaohs of ancient Egypt,
Wouldn't *that* be amazing? That's why
I'm a vegetarian, you see. Because if we do
Have other lives than this, if we return

[63]

In other forms, who's to say we're necessarily
Human each time round? You might have been a cat,
For instance, that would explain your *tours-en-l'aire*.

NIJINSKY

Why is it women seem unable to *think*?
Is it genetic, or does their casual acceptance
Of fantasy as fact spring from having played
With dolls, while boys are drilled in a quick grasp
Of vector quantities?

GLADYS

                              Oh, Vaslav, please—
Not math.

NIJINSKY

                    There, you're doing it,
Acting the role of the gold-digging ditz
Too dumb to number the rings on her fingers
And bells on her toes.

GLADYS

                              I liked you better
When you were a rose.

NIJINSKY

                              It's not as though
Dancers were exempted from the laws
That govern the collisions of planets
And of molecules. Look, when I pirouette,
Then draw my leg closer to my torso, so,
My spin picks up speed. Physics and math
Are not arcane. The wisdom of Euclid
And Pythagoras is carved into the calcium
Of our bones, welded to the iron of our blood.

GLADYS

Then there must be another level of being,
Larger than planets or smaller than molecules,
Where the soul may go, as to a dressing room,
To change the clothing of its flesh. Ballet
Is not, not, not about our physicality.

Ballet is love! When you kiss me,
Surely you aren't thinking what a nice piece
Of meat you have in your mouth, how much
More succulent than sirloin.

                    NIJINSKY
                                        Let us
Put it to the test.

                    GLADYS
                                Vaslav! Be serious!

*Nijinsky kisses Gladys passionately. Music from Wag-
ner's* Tristan.

                    NIJINSKY
Adenine!

                    GLADYS
Guanine!

                    NIJINSKY
                                Inevitable.

                    GLADYS
                                    Interlinking.

                    NIJINSKY
O sugary necessity.

                    GLADYS
                                Fated attraction.
We that were, apart, mere purposeless proteins
Become, united, a nucleotide,
Latest links of a millennial chain
That binds us twain to the sun-stirred tides
Of the primal ocean, eternal bouillabaisse,
Parentless parent, patient, procreative
Source of all that hungers and seeks
To connect.

                    [65]

NIJINSKY

           Dearest double-ringed purine!
Adulated adenine! You are the socket!
I am the plug!

GLADYS

           These are my fingers!
This is their glove! I slip into the groove
Necessity has smoothed for me, and my skin
Is soothed by a breeze of spring. Ying
Meets her Yang.

NIJINSKY

           Sturm meets his Drang.

BOTH

Bonded together, never to part,
Guanine to adenine, as Camus to Sartre.
Each alone issueless, together the source
Of infinite progeny, love and remorse.

   A bell knells.

BRANGÄNE

  [*offstage*]
You two had better simmer down.
Proteins disintegrate as proteins grow.
Molecules come and molecules go,
And love is part of the passing show.

NIJINSKY

Cytosine!

GLADYS
Thymine!

NIJINSKY

           Sight unseen . . .

GLADYS

           Thine is mine!

NIJINSKY

A pyrimidine paragon.

GLADYS

What care I where I am
While I am with you? Where you of uracil,
Still would I love you, still would my oxygen
Lock to your phosphorous. Across the Aegean
And up through the Bosporus, my galley should sail,
Like a new Cleopatra's.

NIJINSKY

Nuclear energies
Fuel our desire! Fissioning nuclei
Shine from your eyes. Radiant Cytosine!

GLADYS

Thymine, my other self! Mythical twin,
Twining with me in serpentine helices,
Mirror reversing right and left,
Machine of perpetual emotion,
Loom on which the shuttles of my soul
Flash to and fro, genetic spinning jenny,
Sin with me, spin with me
Deoxyribonucleically.

A bell knells. The Mouse enters from stage left.

MOUSE

Well, *someone*'s feeling her Cheerios!
I hate to be a party pooper, but that bell's tolling
For you. It's time to wind on down the road.

GLADYS

I'm staying with Vaslav! You'll never move me!
As long as I have life and breath—

MOUSE

But you have neither: had you forgot?
I'll tell you what, I'll help you change
Your mind as easily as shifting gears.
Just step over by these smoking mirrors. . . .

[67]

Gladys allows herself to be led before the largest Mylar panel.

GLADYS

There's no reflection.

MOUSE
                                        Because these mirrors
Reveal the voids and vacancies
Interleaving our lives. In death
Matter matters less and less, as breath
By breath our flesh is sublimated into air,
And that air itself is rarefied to ether.
Here all the zeroes of Arabia
Glisten like dew-sequined blossoms
On the tree of night. *Capisce?*

GLADYS

Not a word. Indeed, while you've been speaking,
I think I've disappeared.

MOUSE
                                        No, only grown
Smaller, diminishing to your atomic height.
I'll follow you at c, the speed of light!

The Mouse steps through the Mylar panel, from which there issues a blinding burst of light.

FOURTH TABLEAUX
The nucleus of an atom, composed of large inflated balloons, on which the Corpse and the Mouse recline, as on a hemispherical waterbed. From time to time an electron speeds through the enveloping darkness in the form of a television monitor. The Corpse has reverted to his original male format.

CORPSE
[*sings*]
Suppose the West's declined already.
Suppose the gathered rose is sick,

The cupboard bare, the limbs unsteady
That once were capable and quick.

Yet still will positrons obey
Nature's eternal protocols,
The same tomorrow as they are today
For atoms as for basketballs.

Still will swift electrons spin
In faery rings about their nuclei,
Their beauty intrinsic and not in
Any beholder's beholding eye.

Do not mourn, therefore, the loss
Of a planet's cast-off clothes.
History's a coverlet of moss
To mantle drunkards' oaths.

MOUSE

Here in the so much simpler realm
Of subatomic particles, we have arrived
At the Jerusalem foretold by the prophets
From Paul to Nietzsche, a *Götterdämmerung*
Without wrong or right, where light's not polarized
In days and nights, but restless vacillates
In troughs and crests. Here the tangled yarn
Of history becomes as clear a tale
As that of Oedipus or Peter Rabbit,
No labyrinth but a simple repeating
Greek-key motif along the hem
Of the millennium. Shall I unfold
A mystery? Then listen as electrons speak!

ELECTRON

[*appearing as a talking head in the TV that flies by
above the atom's nucleus*]
Half-lives had we who ran half-hearted-
Or unmindfully the race that's to be run
Against time's tireless tortoises.
Neglecting our principia, obeying venal
Princes, we died before we could be senile,

[69]

And though still we seemed to live,
We had decayed from radium to lead.

CORPSE

Was that really *Achilles* on TV?

MOUSE

One cannot say of any electron that it is
Precisely anyone at any given moment.
Like our imaginations, or good actors,
Their identities are liquid. See,
Already it has changed channels.

ELECTRON
[a new head on the screen]
Brighter and brighter, the fat's in the fire,
The bombs fall down, and masses expire:
Mere anarchy is loosed upon the world.

Tighter and tighter, the knot of the wire's
Secured by the fingers of Einstein and Teller,
While down in the cellar the wine turns to blood.

Wave and particle, particle and wave,
Let who can save himself himself now save.
To the rest best regards and an unmarked grave.

CORPSE

If I were larger than I have become, as big
As a gene or a gnat, I might be moved by such
Knelling of the bell of nuclear doom. But now
I'm *not* for whom that bell tolls. I'm free
Of all Befores and Afters. Where's my remote?
  [aims beeper at TV]
No more *News of the World!* I cast my vote
For *Death-Styles of the Rich and Famous!*

ELECTRON
[a new head, speaking in the accents of Robin Leach]
Welcome, particles one and all,
To the odd environs of Heisenberg Hall.
Built at simply staggering expense,

Defying reason and confounding sense,
This masterpiece of mathematics
Has seven million meta-attics
Each equipped with a cloud chamber and a bath
Designed according to the highest math.
So *chic* is it, so *très exquise*,
Eye cannot see it, nor can hand squeeze,
For if a single particle of light
Should strike its turrets, it would take flight,
And before you've said, "I think it's there,"
It would be off, you'd know not where.
Thus to the naked human eye
Heisenberg Hall is only fence and sky,
A vision of what might have been
If hand could touch what to the eye's unseen.

CORPSE

How beautiful! How new! In such a house
I'd be content to be the merest mouse.
No slight intended.

MOUSE
And none taken.
Are you all right? You do seem shaken.

CORPSE

For a moment there I thought I saw
A glint, a flicker, a flash, a hint
Of something curiously like . . . me!
But of such strangeness and such charm—

A buzzer sounds twice, and two birds bearing placards saying "Strangeness" and "Charm" come down on wires, after the manner of You Bet Your Life.

MOUSE
The secret words!

CORPSE
And secret worlds
Are opened to our view.

[71]

MOUSE

This atom, too.

The nucleus splits, and its constituent balloons bounce off into the wings and out into the audience. The Corpse and the Mouse sink exit via a trapdoor beneath the splitting atom.

FIFTH TABLEAU

A void. Very quiet music from a gamelan orchestra. The allegorical figures of Strangeness (the Corpse in a white robe) and Charm (the Mouse, unmasked and dressed for tennis) enter, and address the audience antiphonally.

STRANGENESS AND CHARM

Strangeness am I.

And I'm charm.

Together we embody

Something that cannot exist

But does: heads

Without tails, spin

Without mass, either

Without an or,

After *sans* before.

STRANGENESS

All that heretofore has seemed mysterious
We'll now be able to explain.

CHARM

To wit: he's daft, and I'm delirious.

Strangeness regards Charm reproachfully.

CHARM

I'm sorry. I see we must be serious.

STRANGENESS

[*hieratically*]
Quantum and Qabbalah together comprise
The high Platonic propylaeum

To what our physicists denominate
The Eightfold Way, whereon
One melds in Three, and Three's subsumed in Two,
And every Number finds its proper Form,
A snowflake in the heavens' systematic storm.

CHARM

Or dewdrop (the comparison's as apt)
Fallen on a daisy's lenient lap.
We count the petals: *loves me . . . loves me not . . .*
Baryon and burial, hadron and hard-on,
Each one congruent with a thought
In the all-connecting mind of Murray Gell-Mann,
Time's last cosmogonist, atomic Dante.
Welcome, Strangeness, to his game of three-shell monte.
    [*revealing a cardboard with three shells on it, which
    he begins rapidly to slide about*]
Beneath one shell's the small green pea
Inscribed with your next identity.
Beneath the other two is *niente,*
Nothing, *nada, Nichts, rien.*
This one? Or this? Or this? Say when.

    *Strangeness points to one of the shells. Charm lifts it.
    The lights flare to their brightest and then go black.*

VISITORS

Katha Pollitt

The senile bat with nicotine-streaked hair
hefting and sniffing cantaloupes at Key Food—
where had I seen before
that look, shrewd, absorbed, like a bird with a seed?

Of course. And I almost cried out "Madame
Champrigand!" Who taught us girls *Topaze*
and the *belle logique* of the parimutuel system—
and there was a long pause

before I thought, *but she's been dead for years*.
This happens not infrequently—more often
too as I get older—the dead appear
not, as you might imagine,

to startle us with fear or guilt or grief
or the cold fact of our own mortality,
but just to take pleasure again in everyday life:
to walk the dog, or stand in line for a movie,

or pick up a quart of milk and the Sunday *Times*.
Why shouldn't they have an outing? All the same,
it must embarrass them to use their day
passes in such a modest way

which is why when we glimpse them they quickly
dart round the corner or step behind a tree
or cleverly melt into strangers. Only you,
loved shade, do I never see

across the traffic or ahead in the surge of shoppers
swept off into the just-closing elevator door.
Was life so bitter, then, that even these
innocent errands cannot lure you here

for just one afternoon? I would not speak
even your name, you would not have to see me
shadow you drifting down the sunny sidewalk
happy and idle, free. And when you came

at last to the dark and silent subway stairwell
I would not cry or insist. For I would know
you finally: separate, as you were, yourself.
I would not keep you. I would let you go.

THE RIDDLE OF ASMAHAN

Philip Mansel

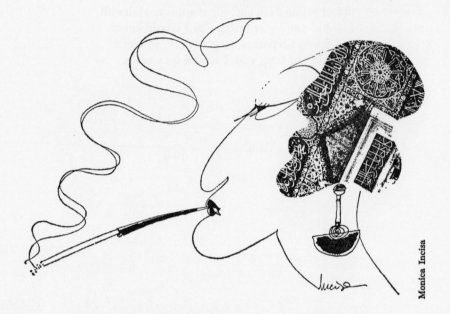

Monica Incisa

During the Second World War, a beautiful princess spied for Britain, sang like an angel, danced naked in the King David Hotel and died in a mysterious car accident. Her name was Asmahan.

She was a Druze, a member of a secretive offshoot of Islam founded in Cairo a thousand years ago by the Caliph al-Hakim bi Amr Allah. His followers thought he was God, and he persecuted Muslims, Jews and Christians with ferocity. The Druzes, now concentrated in Lebanon, Syria and Israel, are different from other Muslims. They believe in reincarnation, can have only one wife at a time and do not pray in the direction of Mecca. The secrets of their faith are enshrined in seven holy books (two are missing, believed to be in England) which can be read only by "the initiated."

Druze women possess more rights than Muslim women.

They can be "initiated," can inherit property to the exclusion of equally qualified males and are less easy to divorce. Sitt Nazira, known as "the veiled lady of Moukhtara," led the powerful Druze clan of Jumblatt in Lebanon from 1921 until 1943. Asmahan was to have an even more unconventional career.

To one of her British admirers, she was "just a Druze peasant," but she was born into the powerful family of the Al-Atrash in 1912: her real name was Emilie (in Arabic, Amal). Her father, the Emir Fahd Farhan al-Atrash, came from the black volcanic region south of Damascus, called the Jebel Druze, or Druze Mountain, because so many Druzes live there. The al-Atrash were Jebel Druze leaders, and in 1925 Asmahan's cousin, Sultan Pasha al-Atrash, who fought with Lawrence of Arabia, became a hero throughout the Arab world when he led a Syrian revolt against the French occupation. The French, who twice bombarded Damascus in order to recover control, regarded the Druzes as mercenaries fomented by the British, France's traditional rivals in the Middle East: Britain did indeed supply arms to the Druzes, who received shelter in British-occupied Transjordan after the failure of the uprising. The Druzes had been pro-British since the 1840s, when a pro-Druze British agent, Colonel Charles Churchill, regarded them as honorary Protestants. Thus Asmahan came from a background which was distinctive, pro-British and favorable to female initiative.

Passion affected Asmahan's life as much as politics. Her Lebanese mother, Aliya, fled from Beirut to Egypt in 1923 with Amal and Amal's brothers, Fouad and Farid, rather than rejoin her unfaithful husband in the Jebel Druze. Fouad al-Atrash remembers the shock of going from a palace to one room, in a Syrian quarter of Cairo called Zaher. They were so poor that their mother had to work as a servant.

After a difficult education (French schools expelled her because of her family's anti-French record), Amal began to sing in 1929 at the age of seventeen, in Madame Badia's Opera Casino, a popular music hall owned by Badia al-Masabni, another woman who had come from Lebanon to seek fame and fortune in Cairo. Amal used the name Asmahan (the name of a pre-Islamic singer who died tragically young). Her first song was called "the fire of my heart and the light of my eyes." For a Druze girl of her class, such a career was outrageous. But Amal was young and poor, and her mother, who sang at private parties to earn money, may have encouraged her. Moreover, Cairo was not Syria. It was relaxed, cosmopolitan and the entertainment capital of the Arab world. Why not?

In 1931, Hassan al-Atrash, hereditary emir (or prince) of the Jebel Druze, came to Cairo, met his second cousins and was bowled over by Asmahan. Equally shocked by her poverty and her career as a public singer (and supported by her conservative brother Fouad, the guardian of "the family honor"), he chose her as his seventh wife; although he was only twenty-six, he had already divorced six times. He took her back to the Jebel Druze. For six years she lived the life of a Druze princess, surrounded by servants. She bore a daughter, Camelia.

There is a saying that once you have tasted the waters of the Nile, you have to return. Suffocated by life in her own community, Asmahan yearned for the bright lights of Cairo. A chance meeting with a Cairo record producer, Dr. Michel Beida, while choosing records in a shop in Damascus, was decisive. Her daughter Camelia was sent to Cairo to see her grandmother, and Asmahan said she wanted to follow. The Emir Hassan loved her but could not persuade her to stay. After violent rows, he agreed to a divorce, provided that he raise their daughter.

When Asmahan returned to Cairo, her brother Farid had already become a famous singer and lute player, as popular in the Arab world as Frank Sinatra in the West. Asmahan herself began to make records—a more respectable, because less public, career than singing in a music hall. She had a good contract because Dr. Beida was in love with her. She then turned to the cinema.

Cairo was Hollywood on the Nile. There were eighteen studios, making films for the entire Arab world: stars earned more, in proportion to the film budget, than in America. At first, for the sake of respectability, Asmahan was the voice-over for other actresses. In 1938, she became famous overnight when she appeared and sang in *The Triumph of Youth*, an autobiographical film about a brother and a sister coming to Egypt from Syria and defying convention by winning fame as musicians. It is one of those Egyptian films, Arab in cast and music yet Western in presentation and style, which confirms that Cairo under King Farouk—who in 1938 was still handsome, popular and full of good intentions—was more modern compared to the rest of the world than it is today. Asmahan told Mohammed Tabi'i, a brilliant Egyptian journalist who had fallen under her spell, "My family will kill me if I appear in a film." But she was seduced by fame, money—and Ahmed Bedrkhan, a writer and film producer with the largest studio in Egypt, Studio Misr, who fell in love and married her. The wedding night, according to another Egyptian director, Henri Barakat, was a disaster. The marriage was dissolved after forty days.

What was Asmahan's secret? Why did Egyptian film producers, Druze princes, and soon French and English generals, fight for her company? She was not conventionally beautiful: she had a prominent nose, a hard chin, short legs and "that pudding face some Druzes have," in the words of Princess Fevzi Osmanoglu. However, her films reveal that she also had the flowing, sleepwalker movements and cold, alluring face of the 1940s siren. In her films she looks like the Marlene Dietrich of the Arab world; she even brandishes a long cigarette holder. In the memoir Mohammed Tabi'i wrote about the love of his life, he admitted she was not beautiful. "But her eyes, her eyes, that was enough. In her eyes were magic, secrets and fascination. They were dark green, with a bit of blue [others claim they were black with a greenish tinge]. Asmahan, God bless her, knew how to use her eyes when necessary." A future Governor-General of New Zealand, General Sir Bernard Fergusson, emphasized another attraction: "Of course, the most remarkable thing about Asmahan are her *dents de loup*. She looks like Dracula's granddaughter."

Asmahan's voice was as unforgettable as her eyes, and because of it she remains a household name in the Arab world today. Passionate, deep and sad, her songs mixed

Arab and Western techniques: one of her most famous
songs, about dancing by night in Vienna, has a waltz
rhythm. Some Arabs believe that with time and training,
Asmahan's voice would have surpassed that of the more
traditional Umm Kulthoum, the most popular singer in
the Arab world: "Asmahan was an aristocrat, with the
finest voice in Egypt. Umm Kulthoum was a peasant in
comparison."

Asmahan's is the voice of a woman who ignored barriers of class, sex, race and faith in order to lead her own
life: the voice of Cairo in the '40s, when it was one of
the most enthralling cities in the world, at a crossroads
of cultures and empires. At the same time, Cairo was
the site of British headquarters in the Middle East, capital of Egypt, the center of the new forces of Arab nationalism and Muslim fundamentalism and, in the words of
British novelist Olivia Manning, "a bureau of sexual exchange." While princesses gave balls for a thousand,
peasants lived like animals on the royal estates.

Asmahan's heart-rending voice, searchlight eyes and
gale-force personality made her irresistible. Leila Doss,
daughter of a prominent lawyer, remembers Asmahan's
visits to the family house in Cairo: "She was one of those
people you never forget. She was very capable, very
intelligent and very charming. No one could ever control her. Princess Shivekiar offered her a thousand pounds
to sing at one of her parties. She refused, saying she was
tired, and sang in the Café des Pigeons on the Nile instead. All the men would flock around her."

One of those who flocked was Ahmed Hassanein Pasha,
First Chamberlain of King Farouk, the crucial link between the Palace and the British Embassy, the hero of a
hundred political intrigues, the explorer of the lost oases
of the Egyptian desert with Rosita Forbes, a famous
British lady traveler of the 1920s. Hassanein was so
charming that many ladies in Cairo were a little in love
with him; but he was the lover, or morganatic husband,
of King Farouk's mother, Queen Nazli. Tabi'i introduced
him to Asmahan in 1940 or 1941 and claims that Asmahan
loved Hassanein until she died. King Farouk played her
records at full volume in the gardens of Abdine Palace to

tease his chamberlain. His mother was less amused. One day Hassanein telephoned Asmahan from the palace, saying, "Is it true that I visit you, Madame Atrash? Is it true that you visit me in my house? Thank you, Madame Atrash." She was delighted at the thought of the Queen Mother jealously listening to her denials. Rather than a *coup de foudre*, her marriage to Bedrkhan may have been a tactical move to obtain an Egyptian visa (often refused to foreign entertainers) and prevent her expulsion from Egypt by a government eager to please Queen Nazli. Hassanein's frequent visits to her at the Mena House Hotel beside the Pyramids surprised everyone who knew this normally discreet courtier.

One of Asmahan's greatest allies in extracting the most out of life was Amina al-Barudi, beautiful, uncontrollable (she jumped into the Nile in a fur coat when her lover forgot to kiss her) and rich. She tried to reconcile Asmahan and Ahmed Bedrkhan, but he was unjustly convinced

Monica Incisa

[81]

that Amina and Asmahan were lovers: "I am not an imbecile! I have eyes in my head!"

Indeed, despite the number and ardor of her male admirers and her apparent devotion to Hassanein, Asmahan may have preferred women: there were rumors of a close relationship with a black servant. Her mother, however, said that she was fundamentally hard and loved no one but herself. And forty years later, after the war, drinking gin and tonic in the Travellers Club in Paris, a British officer remembers: "I don't think there were many orgasms in her life. . . . Not much purpose in life, you know. She loved to have a table of friends sitting around her, and to be the center of attention, naturally."

Although courtiers might be gossiping about the First Chamberlain's visits to the Mena House Hotel, most people in Cairo had other topics of conversation. In May 1941, the kings of Yugoslavia and Greece also moved into the Mena House Hotel: their countries were now occupied by the German army. Britain was alone against the Axis. German and Italian troops were advancing on Cairo from the western desert, and many Arabs were praying for their victory. A shared hostility to the British and the Jews, and the brilliant *Greet the Arabs* radio programs broadcast from Berlin, convinced Arabs that Hitler ("Abu Ali") was a friend. A popular song that year went:

> No more Monsieur, no more Mister!
> Go away, get out of here!
> We want Allah in heaven and Hitler on earth.

A pro-German government came to power in Iraq on April 1, 1941. The entire British position in the Middle East was in the balance. Would Syria and Lebanon, still occupied by French forces loyal to the pro-German Vichy government, be the next to go? Rahn, a redoubtable and charming German agent who flew into Aleppo in northern Syria on May 9, persuaded or ordered General Dentz, the French commander-in-chief in Syria, to allow German planes to refuel on Syrian airstrips and to dispatch massive quantities of French munitions to Iraq. Britain, hav-

ing recovered control of Iraq by the end of May, decided
to invade Syria.

Britain needed the Druzes for their military prowess
and for their geographical position—on the route of any
force invading Syria from British-occupied Transjordan
in the south. John Glubb, commander of the Arab Legion
in Transjordan, and Alec Kirkbride, British minister in Amman, distorting official British policy, offered money and,
ultimately, independence from the French if the Druzes
helped Britain. On May 20, General Archibald Wavell,
the British commander-in-chief in the Middle East, reported that Druze and native troops "have declared will-
ing to act as advanced screen to advancing Free French
forces to avoid attacks by native population" (the last
phrase confirms German propaganda's success in Syria).

The British authorities in Cairo feared that the excellent German spy network in Syria, controlled by a Ges-
tapo representative called Roser and his assistant, Paula
Koch, might convince or bribe the Druzes—who had recently been given considerable autonomy by France—to
oppose the British. Mohammed Tabi'i went to the same
nightclub as a British officer and introduced him to Asmahan. Such a direct link to the leader of the Jebel Druzes
had to be exploited. Brigadier Iltid Clayton of British
Military Intelligence decided to use Asmahan to convince
or bribe the Emir Hassan to support Britain against the
Vichy French. On May 24, Asmahan told Tabi'i, laughing,
that she was being paid £40,000 to go on a secret mission
to Syria: "You always thought I was useless. Now I will
show you. I am serving my country. Hassan al-Atrash still
loves me and often adopted my opinion when I was his
wife. I do not think it will be difficult to convince them."

She thus added the roles of British spy and Syrian
nationalist to her already impressive array of personalities:
Druze princess and Egyptian film star, defenseless orphan
and *femme fatale*. She was able to play so many parts in
so few years because the normal code of behavior of her
class, race and sex meant nothing to her. Believing the
fortune-teller who had told her that she would die at the
age of thirty-two, she wanted to break all the rules and
push life to the limits.

In the next weeks she did more than most people manage in a lifetime. Claiming she had been expelled from Egypt for holding gambling parties, she moved to Jerusalem, where Churchill's niece Anita Leslie found her singing to Arab chiefs and Free French officers and establishing extremely close relations with her British liaison officers, Major Aly Khan (there were many Ismaili followers of his father, the Aga Khan, in Syria) and Major Randolph Churchill. Like Lawrence of Arabia in the First World War, she worked for a special intelligence unit called the Arab Bureau, which was set up in Jerusalem on May 26. In Amman, Kirkbride, the British minister, was appalled by Asmahan, "laughing vivaciously" in badly cut riding breeches, and refused to be seen in the same car. He wrote in his memoirs that her presence was "entirely unnecessary." However, he did take her to meetings on the frontier, where he noticed that the moment an elderly Druze sheikh appeared "Asmahan became a Druze woman again, kissed his hand and retired in silence into the background."

On May 28, only four days after leaving Cairo, she drove to the Orient Palace Hotel in Damascus, where she met the Emir Hassan, who once more fell under her spell, divorced his current wife, Hind Alameddine, and remarried Asmahan. The quantities of gold sovereigns she distributed helped to silence Druze doubts about her morality and win Druze support for Britain. She used discreet encounters at the bar of the Orient Palace Hotel to meet Druze and Syrian leaders. Lieutenant Karkoutly, then in French Military Security, remembers that she made secret journeys back to Jerusalem to report on the opinions of Syrian politicians and the state of French defenses, slipping through the Golan Heights disguised as a black slave. She used her sexual freedom as a weapon, placating an inquisitive soldier by sleeping with him. She helped to ensure that the Druzes did not fight for the Germans and Vichy—as did other Syrians such as the legendary anti-British guerilla leader Fawzi al-Kaoukgi.

In the middle of the hottest summer for fifty years, on June 8, 1941, without a declaration of war, British, Commonwealth and Free French troops invaded Syria—the last occasion in history when French and British armies fought each other, and one of the less glorious campaigns of the modern British army. Large Vichy French forces were posted to northern Syria to deter Turkish plans of expansion, and news of increased German demands on occupied France had arrived. Nevertheless, the Vichy troops fought ferociously, in Rahn's opinion better than the British. The promised rallying of Vichy troops to the Free French did not occur; indeed, clashes between the forces of Pétain and de Gaulle were especially vicious. The British were grateful for the help of a Druze legion raised in Palestine and of the irregular Druze cavalry—one of the last cavalry forces to operate in modern warfare.

Finally, on June 21, allied troops entered Damascus—one day before German troops swept into Russia. Wearing the dazzling white *mandil*, the cloak of the Atrash ladies, and clutching a goatskin bag of gold sovereigns, Asmahan made a sensation at the victory parade through Damascus on July 3. An armistice, strangely lenient for the Vichy French, was signed on July 14. It says much about French feelings and prospects of a British victory that, in July 1941, only 5,668 of 37,736 French soldiers in Syria chose to join the Free French and fight beside the British. Most preferred to be shipped back to their families in rationed, defeated, German-occupied France.

Having defeated the Vichy French, the British and the Free French turned on each other. The head of the British mission to the Free French in the Levant was General Louis Spears. Witty, ambitious, speaking perfect French, as Churchill's personal representative in the dark days of the fall of France he had selected de Gaulle as the officer most likely to help the allied cause and flown him to England. The Middle East has the power to envenom and dramatize any relationship, and that between Spears and de Gaulle and their forces was no exception. The Druzes were at the center of the row.

The Jebel Druze was still controlled by Colonel Bouvier, a Pétainiste who used it to divide the British and the Free French. There was a British plan (and there had been British promises) to separate this traditionally independent and pro-British region from Syria. Emir Has-

san and Emira Amal helped to persuade Bouvier and his
forces to leave without fighting on July 24; British troops
were welcomed with joy, and the Union Jack was raised
on the French Residency in Suweida, capital of the Jebel
Druze. To de Gaulle it seemed that the British were taking advantage of the Second World War to dismember
the French Empire. Free French forces marched on Suweida from Damascus and surrounded it on July 29. A
battle appeared inevitable. In the end, the British backed
down and evacuated the area of the Jebel Druze. Their
dreams of Druze independence (or union with Transjordan) were foiled.

Once, in the words of an officer on Spears's staff, "an
important element in our political plans," Asmahan
was now dispensable: the Free French remained in Syria
until their final departure in 1945, after many clashes
with the British and the Druzes. In 1941, Anita Leslie
found Asmahan looking rather pathetic in her husband's
house in Suweida, filled with Waring and Gillow furniture. Her only joy came from a cocktail bar she had had
installed, where she mixed the drinks herself: she was
reputedly able to drink any man under the table.

However, Asmahan still had sex as a weapon. In one
of the most romantic passages in the memoirs of a modern British general, Spears wrote: "She was and always
will be to me one of the most beautiful women I have
ever seen. Her eyes were immense, green as the color of
the sea you have to cross on the way to paradise. . . . She
bowled over British officers with the accuracy and speed
of a machine gun" (*Fulfillment of a Mission*, 1977). At
a tea party given at Ain Sofar in the mountains above
Beirut in August 1941, an officer on Spears's staff wrote:
"Among those there, looking extremely beautiful in an
Arab headdress, was the Emira al-Atrash." There was a
dramatic contrast between the decorous party and the
vicious feuds smoldering among the British, French and
Arab guests. Asmahan, who had been divorced for the
second time by Emir Hassan, was escorted by her superior
in the Arab Bureau, Air Commander Buss, who was both
her paymaster—she received £400 per month—and her
lover. They wore each other's hats. She lost her lover and

her salary at the same time when Oliver Lyttelton, British Minister of State in the Middle East, expelled Buss from Syria for indecorous behavior. At dinner with General Spears, Asmahan told a British officer: *Je déteste ma vie.*

A friend from these days in Beirut, Madame de Serres, remembers Asmahan often returning from parties completely drunk: "She had an enormous appetite for power and luxury. She was all woman, she knew how to manipulate men." Asmahan was so confident of her ability to manipulate men—and governments—that, like many Arabs, including the future President Sadat (and the Druze leaders Shakib and Adil Arslan), she turned to Germany. The British authorities learned that she had obtained a visa for neutral Turkey, where there was an extensive German spy network. In September 1941 she slipped out of Beirut in the boot of a car belonging to a fat and charming pro-Vichy American journalist called Mr. Violette (the United States was still neutral). The British let her leave in order to draw out pro-German agents who might help her journey; the Syrian railways and the Levant Express Trading Company of Beirut were full of them. However, just as Sadat, then fanatically anti-British, was prevented from reaching the Germans when his plane crashed, so Asmahan was arrested at the Turkish frontier by a British officer while the engine on the Taurus Express going from Aleppo to Ankara was being changed. He claimed, falsely, that there were British troops behind the hills surrounding the train, and she must leave.

"She bit me on the arm, she kicked me for quite a long time. She was with Georgette Cafoury, a cowardly little Lebanese who peed in her pants whenever anything went wrong." In the end she believed the Briton's story. Such was her magnetism that, although she had been planning to betray British secrets to the Germans, she was entertained that night by her British captors in the Cercle d'Orient in Aleppo: she was seen as an independent agent and "it never occurred to us to be angry." Lieutenant Karkaoutly remembers that the party was also used to extract the last secrets, before his execution, of a German agent called Jelal Latifeh.

For a time Asmahan endured *résidence forcée* in Beirut, in a villa whose rent was shared by the British and the Free French. An Armenian merchant gave her another villa in the mountains out of gratitude for help with a problem over an import licence. She could still mow down men. Among her admirers were General John (known as Jack) Evetts, commander of the Sixth Division, so besotted that he had to be sent back to England; "Sim" Feversham, a Lord in Waiting to King George VI and an officer in the Household Cavalry; Major Hope, head of British Military Security in Damascus; and Brigadier Buller of the Transjordan Frontier Force. General Georges Catroux gave her her own Druze *garde d'hon-*

Monica Incisa

neur, which was enlarged for parties. Officers enjoyed going to see her (the higher their rank, the warmer their welcome), but often had the feeling that there was one man hidden behind the door, another in a cupboard and a third under the bed. British ladies called her not Princess al-Atrash but Princess Trash. They blamed her success on the lack of competition, and are said to have sent a written request to the military authorities to stop their husbands' seeing her.

Jerusalem, then the pleasant cosmopolitan capital of undivided Palestine, was her next home. She lived in a suite above GHQ in the King David Hotel. Amina al-Barudi came from Egypt to keep her company, and they shared the same room. "Having breakfast with those girls was quite an experience. . . . My God, they were wonderful company. They had an extraordinary dovetailing effect. They set each other off." Another visitor to the King David Hotel was Asmahan's rival, Queen Nazli—to whom she lent her suite. Spears was told that Asmahan presided over orgies. "She would do a strip-tease act and, when a state of complete nudity had been achieved, would dance with specially selected British officers."

Such license when so many Druzes lived nearby was very bold. As Robert Benton Betts writes in his excellent study, *The Druze* (Yale University Press, 1988): "It is not unknown even today for a Druze woman who has shamed her family to be murdered by her nearest male relative." Asmahan's husband and other relations were said to have agents at the Lebanese frontier, waiting to kill her.

While in Jerusalem she was offered a splendid contract by Ahmad Salim, a director of Studio Misr, and husband of the most famous belly-dancer in Cairo, the beautiful Tahiya Carioca (known as "Gyppy Tummy"). Asmahan's goatskin bag of British sovereigns was beginning to feel rather light; she was being dropped as an embarrassment by her British admirers; so she signed. In order to gain an Egyptian passport to fulfill her contract, she married Ahmad Salim. She liked him because he teased her and did not treat her as a Druze princess. Tahiya Carioca returned to Jerusalem from a tour in Syria to find she had lost her husband.

Back in Egypt, Asmahan was given £3,000 and a villa next to the newly opened nightclub, the Auberge des Pyramides—unprecedented rewards for an actress. She began work on her best film, *Love and Vengeance*, about a fatal love for a beautiful singer. Her separate lives continued. She was taken to fashionable restaurants in Cairo and Alexandria such as Le P'tit Coin de France or Pastroudis by Hussein Said, director of the Alexandria tramways, or Victor Simaica, a celebrated man about town. Like most Egyptians, Simaica was unimpressed by her Syrian background and adventures. He remembers: "She was an attractive woman, but there were so many in Cairo in those days. She always struck me as a nice girl, simple, direct. She had the flat head of the Syrians. No one took her seriously as a princess." Asmahan, who rarely went to grand private parties ("She was never admitted to any part of Society"), used to sing at charity fetes in the presence of King Farouk, from a white marble platform in the middle of the pool in the dreamlike Ottoman Italian palace of Shoubra, on the edge of Cairo.

Although Asmahan applied to the conduct of her marriage the skills learned as a spy in Syria, the marriage soon deteriorated. Ahmed Salim, a great *coureur de femmes* himself, who had been tried for supplying the Egyptian army with defective helmets, refused to let her come home at three in the morning and made a scene if she put the phone down when he entered the room. One day he saw her leave Hassanein's house and demanded an explanation. The First Chamberlain, always suave, said: "Ahmed, you are my son, and your wife is like my daughter. I am fascinated by her voice like everyone else." Asmahan said, "I visit whom I like when I like. If you don't agree, divorce me." There were rows, gun shots, he tried to strangle her. She called the neighbors, the police and a local imam. She screamed at her husband, "I can't live with you because you want my money for gambling."

One of the mysteries of Asmahan is that she appears independent and alluring in retrospect, but seemed aimless and awkward to her friends. She would shut herself up in her room and cry for hours, or visit graveyards and talk to the dead. Worried by the impending breakup of her marriage, she decided to go for a rest to Ras al-Bar, a resort on the Mediterranean where fashionable Egyptians relaxed in villas made of straw. (The beaches of Alexandria were closed for the duration of the war.)

Monica Incisa

She left on July 14, 1944, with her companion Marie
Glada and Ahmed Salim's chauffeur, not in the elegant
white Cord given to her by Emir Hassan but in a car
from Misr Studios. In a small village between Talha and
Mansourah, the car sped off the road and sank in the
water—on a spot where a similar accident had almost
happened to her four years earlier. She and Marie Glada
were drowned; the chauffeur, Mohammed Fadlalah, survived. Her funeral was attended by a crowd of celebrities;
Love and Vengeance was changed to incorporate a fatal
car accident as its climax.

Most people believed, and Spears (who visited the
scene of her death) implies in his memoirs, that the chauffeur was paid to fix her death by one of the forces com-
peting for control of Egypt: the King, the British or, in
the shape of her own husband or family, traditional religion. Were British agents so alarmed by the contract
she had signed with an American publisher to write her
memoirs that they arranged for a quiet liquidation, like
that of the inconveniently pro-Pétain Admiral Darlan
two years before, in Algiers? Did she know too much
about the private life of the Egyptian royal family? Did
she go too far for the Druzes? One of the most famous
journalists in Egypt, Mustafa Amin, disagrees. Sitting in
the office whence he still controls his newspaper *Al Akh-
bar* at the age of eighty, he says: "It was an accident. I
investigated the incident. . . . The car jumped into the
canal."

Since Asmahan's death, her world has disappeared. The British Empire in the Middle East is a distant memory. The cosmopolitan Levantine cities where Asmahan danced and sang have been made unrecognizable by nationalism and fanaticism. Beirut has been destroyed. Jerusalem seethes with hate. Much of central Cairo, including Madame Badia's Opera Casino, was burnt on Black Saturday, January 26, 1952, by infuriated nationalistic crowds (Madame Badia retired to the Lebanese countryside, where she was said to dance in front of her cows to get them to produce more milk). Six months later, a military *coup d'état* overthrew King Farouk and ushered in the age of Nasser and nationalism. Hassanein, who might have prevented the King's degeneration, had also died in a car crash in 1946. Barriers between religions and communities are stronger than ever in the Middle East today. Asmahan's world and friends have taken refuge in the last strongholds of the Levant: London and Paris.

The power of the Al-Atrash has been broken by a series of brutal Syrian governments. The Jebel Druze is now called the Jebel Arab; the al-Atrash mansion in Suweida is the local headquarters of the Ba'ath Arab Socialist party. Only in Lebanon does Druze power survive, in a semi-independent state south of Beirut, with its own port and army, dominated by Walid Jumblatt, a nephew of the Emir Hassan. The Emir Hassan, after a tempestuous political career, died from the effects of a time in prison in 1977: his ninth and last wife had been murdered by unidentified gunmen the year before. His daughter by Asmahan, Camelia, is happily married and leads as quiet a life as is possible in modern Lebanon: she rarely talks about her mother.

Her brother, Farid al-Atrash, made thirty-one films and died in 1974, at the height of his fame. The surviving brother, Fouad, lives in a flat overlooking the Nile, with Arabesque ceilings and with walls and cupboards overflowing with framed photographs, including one of General de Gaulle looking unusually relaxed beside Asmahan. Fouad is slightly ashamed of his sister, but occasionally pride and nostalgia triumph: *"Nous sommes une famille royale, une famille royale! Nous sommes pour tout le monde. Elle était grande amie avec les anglais . . ."*

Monica Incisa

CONTEMPORARY CULTURE AND
THE LETTER 'K'

Alfred Corn

First inroads were made in our 19-aughts
(Foreshadowed during the last century by nothing
More central than "Kubla Khan," Kipling, Greek
Letter societies, including the grotesque KKK—
Plus the kiwi, koala, and kookaburra from Down Under)
When certain women applied to their moist eyelids
A substance pronounced *coal* but spelled *kohl*,
Much of the effect captured on Kodak film
With results on and off camera now notorious.
They were followed and sometimes chased by a platoon
Of helmeted cutups styled the *Keystone Kops*, who'd
Freeze in the balletic pose of the letter itself
Left arm on hip, leg pointed back at an angle,
Waiting under klieg lights next to a worried kiosk
To put the kibosh on Knickerbocker misbehavior.
Long gone, they couldn't help when that hirsute royal
King Kong arrived to make a desperate last stand,
Clinging from the Empire State, swatting at biplanes,
Fay Wray fainting away in his leathern palm
As in the grip of African might. Next, marketing
Stepped up with menthol tobacco and the brand name
Kool, smoked presumably by models and archetypes
Superior in every way to Jukes and Kallikaks.
By then the race was on, if only because
Of German *Kultur*'s increasing newsworthiness
On the international front. The nation that had canned
Its Kaiser went on to sponsor debuts for the hero
Of *Mein Kampf*, Wotan of his day, launching thunderbolts
And Stukkas, along with a new social order astonishing
In its industrial efficiency. His annexing
Of Bohemia cannot have been spurred by reflecting
That after all Prague had sheltered the creator
And in some sense alter ego of Josef K.,
Whose trial remained a local fact until the fall
Of the Empire of a Thousand Years, unheard of in "Amerika"
Of the Jazz Age. But musicians Bix Beiderbecke and Duke

Ellington somehow always took care to include the token
Grapheme in their names, for which precaution fans
Of certain priceless 78s can only be grateful.
They skipped and rippled through a long postwar glow
Still luminous in the memory of whoever recalls
Krazy Kat, Kleenex, Deborah Kerr, Korea, Kool-Aid,
And Jack Kennedy. Small wonder if New York had
A special feeling for the theme, considering radical
Innovations of de Kooning, Kline, and Rothko. This last
Can remind us that bearers of the letter often suffered
Bereavement and despair (*cf.* Chester Kallman) and even,
As with Weldon Kees, self-slaying. Impossible not to see
Symptoms of a malaise more widespread still in a culture
That collects kitsch and Krugerrands, with a just-kids lifestyle
Whose central shrine is the shopping mall—K-Mart, hail to thee!
To "Kuntry Kitchen," "Kanine Kennels," and a host of other
Kreative misspellings kreeping through the korpus
Of kontemporary lingo like an illness someone someday
(The trespass of metaphor) is going to spell "kancer."

True, there have been recidivists in opposite
Direction (a falling away perhaps from the Platonic ideal
Of *tò kalón**) like "calisthenics" and Maria Callas,
Who seem to have preferred the less marblelike romance
Of traditional English. This and related factors make all
Supporters of the letter "k" in legitimate forms
And avatars cherish it with fiery intensity—
All the more when besieged by forces beyond
Anyone's control, at least, with social or medical
Remedies now available. Dr. Kaposi named it,
That sarcoma earmarking a mortal syndrome thus far
Incurable and spreading overland like acid rain.
A sense of helplessness is not in the repertory
Of our national consciousness, we have no aptitude
For standing by as chill winds rise, the shadows gather,
And gray light glides into the room where a seated figure
Has taken up his post by the window, facing away from us,
No longer bothering to speak, his mind at one with whatever
Is beyond the ordinary spell of language, whatever dreams us
Into that placeless place, its nearest image a cloudless
Sky at dusk, just before the slow ascent of the moon.

* *tò kalón*: Greek, "the beautiful."

FANTASIA ON THE RELATIONS BETWEEN POETRY AND PHOTOGRAPHY

Mark Strand

I

ON THE SADNESS OF A FAMILY PHOTOGRAPH

I have a photograph of my mother, my sister and myself, taken when I was about four years old and when my mother was thirty-two or so. My sister and I are standing on what must be the front walk of our house then, in front of a hedge, and my mother is crouched in the middle with an arm around each of us. It must be spring, because I am wearing shorts and a long-sleeved shirt, which is buttoned, probably as a concession to neatness, at the neck. My sister, who was then about two and a half, is wearing a coat that stops just above her knees. The sleeves are too long. It must be noon or close to it; our common shadow is directly beneath us. My mother's hair is dark and she is smiling. The light spills over her forehead and rides the top of her cheeks, a patch of it rests on one side of her chin. The light falls the same way over my sister's face and mine. And the eyes of all three of us are in shadow in precisely the same way. I have stared and stared at this photograph, and each time I have felt a deep and inexplicable rush of sadness. Is it that my mother, who holds us and one of whose hands I hold, is now dead? Or is it that she is so young, so happy, so proud of her children? Is it that the three of us are momentarily bound by the way the light distributes itself in identical ways over each of our faces, binding us together, proclaiming our unity for a moment in a past that was just ours and that no one now can share? Or is it simply that we look a bit out of date? Or that whatever we were at the moment catches the heart merely by being over? I suppose all are good reasons for feeling sad, and they may account in some part for my feelings, but there is something else that I am responding to. It is the presence of the photographer. He is the one by whom the three of us in the photograph are so powerfully moved. It is for him that my mother allows herself to be so spontaneously present, to show an aspect of herself uncomplicated by any withholding, any sign of sorrow. And it is towards him that I lean, to him that I want to run. It is not being photographed that is important to me, it is the taker of the photograph. But who was he? He must have been my father, I keep saying to myself, my father who, in those days, seemed always absent, always on the road, selling one of the news services to the small-town papers in Pennsylvania. So, it is not that a moment of sweetness was and will never be again that makes me sad. It is that the one most powerfully present is not in the picture, but exists conjecturally, as an absence. Something else that moves me about this photograph is the way it is so much about the moment in which it was taken. Like childhood itself, it is innocent of the future. I feel an enormous sympathy for the small boy I was, and I feel guilty that his likeness should be served up years later to his older self; I existed, at that moment, not for my gaze today, but for the photographer at the moment of the photograph. In other words, I was not posing. I couldn't, because I could not anticipate a future for that moment; I lived, like most children, in a perpetual present. I could hold still, but I could not pose. And in my holding still, I manifest a tremendous eagerness to break free, to embrace my father who is nowhere in the picture.

II
ON THE SADNESS OF ANOTHER FAMILY PHOTO

I have another photograph of my mother, taken when she was twenty-four. She sits with her mother on the beach in Miami. Neither is in a bathing suit. My grandmother wears a sweater over a blouse and skirt, my mother a dark something-or-other. In the background, a lifeguard sits to the side of a white wooden lookout station with a canvas canopy on top. My mother stares directly into the lens, as if at that second obeying the photographer's request to look at the camera. Why is this such a sad photograph? My mother looks more beautiful than she ever has. And she is smiling. Even her mother, for whom I always heard happiness was unobtainable, seems happy. What then? It is another case of the missing person. And in this photograph, I am the one who is missing. I was not yet born, nor conceived, nor had my mother even met my father. That my mother was happily alive despite my absence does not come as any surprise, but on some level it does offer a rebuke to my presence and seems to question my own importance. After all, I knew her only in relation to myself, so there is a part of me that feels left out, even jealous. There is something else, too. I see her not as my mother, but as a beautiful young woman, and I think to myself how I wish I had known her then. For she might have liked me, and I might have liked her. We might even have been lovers. It is the impossibility of this erotic connection that is saddening. For isn't it a way of having her back, of wanting to claim her entirely for myself? I fantasize being alive before I was born. How hopeless. One confronts the absence of self, and such a loss is without sweetness, for it is absolute, for no revision is possible, one cannot rewrite the scenario of one's life when one was not alive. So my mother stares at the camera, which was probably held by her father. She smiles alluringly. She is at that moment a trusting subject. It is a sunny, cloudless day in Miami. But fifty-eight years later a shadow hovers over that moment of brightness, of familial equilibrium. It is I, it is the future, experiencing a terrible, ineradicable exclusion.

III
ON THE DIFFERENCE BETWEEN FAMILY PHOTOS
AND PHOTOS OF THE REST OF THE WORLD

Something about family snapshots sets them apart from photographs of the rest of the world. We look at them differently, feel more passionately about them. They may be of ourselves, no doubt contributing to our greater absorption, but they don't have to be. They can be of anybody we are close to, close enough to so that our emotional ties and shifting affections easily cloud or color our vision of these significant others, leaving us in perpetual doubt as to how they should be seen and making us question whatever views of them we encounter. Family snapshots offer us something like what the French critic Roland Barthes called *punctum*. A punctum is something in the photograph, a detail, that stings or pierces the viewer into an emotional reassessment of what he has seen. It can be a necklace, a flawed smile, the position of a hand—a thing or gesture—that urges itself on us, compels our vision, with sudden, unexpected poignancy. It is not something that can be controlled or anticipated by the photographer, for it is a detail that puts the photograph into a context other than that of its inception. What we experience looking at family snapshots may not be, strictly speaking, what Barthes meant by punctum, but it is related. For often enough we are struck by something in the look of someone we're close to that might tell us more about them and might challenge or confirm the accuracy of our feelings. And often enough the volatility of our needs and expectations changes what we see, turning the images of loved ones into occasions for reverie and the events surrounding them into topics for investigation.

I was being, I admit, a little mischievous when I used the expression "photographs of the rest of the world." After all, the world is large and at least as various as the photographs taken of it. And when I set family snapshots against photographs of the rest of the world, I was creating categories that are based on extremes of experience. I assumed that photographs of the rest of the world do not relinquish themselves to our emotional keep as easily as family pictures. For one thing, we care less about the world than about what goes on at home; for another, we are able to cast ourselves at the center of our domestic scene, but it would be madness to imagine ourselves at the center of the larger one. When confronted with images of the world, we are rarely stung into revisions and reassessments of ourselves in relation to it. We rarely feel the need to come to terms with what already seems fixed or seems understood, however exotic it might be. Our response is likely to be one of passive acceptance. And the visual climate or character of the photograph will prove subservient to a coding that is culturally or historically determined. Even if the photograph reveals terrible social ills, it will not appear unaccountably problematical; instead, it will inevitably provide an allegorical reading to explain itself. Good and evil will be righteously "exposed," and the photograph's appeal, ultimately, will be to our understanding. In other words, such photographs supply a familiar context by which they can be read. The *unac-counted for*, which in family snapshots often amounts to revelation, is merely out-of-place in photographs of the world.

IV

ON POSING AS A DEFENSE AGAINST THE CANDOR OF FAMILY PHOTOGRAPHS

Like photos of the rest of the world, formal photographs, or those in which people pose, resist the kind of personal revelation that family snapshots offer. In fact, it could be said that it is precisely personal revelation that posing is a defense against. The poser wants to transcend the inner-personal climate and context of the family snapshot. He does not want to be discovered as anything other than what he determines. He does not wish to be himself so much as he wishes to be an object, that is, he would rather be judged aesthetically than personally, and the world he would join is the permanent one of art. To look alive, for him, is to look flawed. He has an idea about the way he looks, and he wants it confirmed. So he tries to control the outcome of the picture and to anticipate, as much as he can, what he will look like; but his extreme self-consciousness always results in an image of estrangement—a look of dispassion clouds the eyes, he appears to be elsewhere. His expectations are based on delusive claims that have to do with needs beyond the camera's power to satisfy. For instance, if our poser is haunted by conventional beauty, he may wish to look like a movie star; if he is transported by standard embodiments of responsibility, he may wish to look like a statesman. The point is that he wants the camera to be responsive to an image, not to a self.

So what is the poser afraid of? Why does he wish to appear a particular way and not any old way? Is it just vanity that would have him look perfect instead of himself? Or do his needs have more to do with self-preservation, that is, a refusal to be reminded of his mortality? Either way, the results are the same. His idealization means that he will not be located temporally. When he looks at the photograph years later, he need not feel even a twinge of sadness, nor need we in the event that our poser has died. We cannot rightly mourn his loss for the simple reason that he has not allowed enough of himself in the photograph. Instead, he has become his own ageless memorial.

V

ON RILKE'S POEM 'PORTRAIT OF MY FATHER AS A YOUNG MAN': EVIDENCE OF THE LIMITATIONS OF POSING

When I look at the photograph of my mother and grandmother, I experience a sadness that has to do with my own absence from a period of my mother's life. In other words, I experienced my death in reverse—I was born too late to be there. In the need to locate myself as I study the photograph, I am struck by the arbitrariness of our temporal existence. In Rilke's poem "Portrait of My Father as a Young Man," the painstaking scrutiny of a photograph leads him inescapably to a sense of his own mortality.

PORTRAIT OF MY FATHER AS A YOUNG MAN

In the eyes: dream. The brow as if it could feel
something far off. Around the lips, a great
freshness—seductive, though there is no smile.
Under the rows of ornamental braid
on the slim Imperial officer's uniform:
the saber's basket-hilt. Both hands stay
folded upon it, going nowhere, calm
and now almost invisible, as if they
were the first to grasp the distance and dissolve.
And all the rest so curtained with itself,
so cloudy, that I cannot understand
this figure as it fades into the background—.

Oh quickly disappearing photograph
in my more slowly disappearing hand.

Those hands folded upon the basket-hilt that will go nowhere, that will complete no gesture—neither in the photograph, because it is still, nor in life because the father is dead—are calm as they disappear, forming a kind of retreat from activity, from actuality. The photograph

is fading, everything in it is so cloudy, so curtained with
itself, so removed, in other words, it becomes not a moment that has been rescued, a fragment of life that has
been saved, but an emblem of death. And as if he could
anticipate this at the time the photo was taken, feel the
moment of disintegration approaching, Rilke's father already had begun to disengage himself from the inevitable,
and substitute another remoteness, one generated from
within, the dream whose origins and destiny are more
ethereal, harder to pin down than our features. So, even
when the photo was taken, he was elsewhere, which is why
Rilke has such a hard time locating him. What Rilke encounters in this fading memorial of his father, this mask
from which his father had removed himself, is only a pose,
which is why he says "I cannot understand this figure." In
order to save his father, he must read into the photograph
what it fails to show. Thus "the brow *as if* it could feel
something far off," and "the hands *as if* they could grasp
(that is, close around as well as understand) the distance."
A photograph cannot describe what is not there. But language can, and this is one of the moving features of Rilke's
poem—the desire to know more than the photograph
can possibly record, and the ultimate dependence on the
speculative properties of language to supply it. Language
responds to what is within or behind or hidden, to what,
in other words, is not readily seen, suggesting that just
as dark is the beginning of invention, so light is its con-
clusion. Thus, as the light of the photo fades, the poem
takes over. And if the hand is a metonym for writing, as
it frequently is, then in this poem it assumes the burden
of carrying on, for a while, the image of Rilke's father. But
only for a while, since the poem, too, is mortal.

VI

ON JOHN ASHBERY'S POEM 'MIXED FEELINGS' AND
ITS REJECTION OF THE SORT OF SADNESS OFTEN
ASSOCIATED WITH FAMILY SNAPSHOTS

John Ashbery's poem begins, as Rilke's does, with the
description of a photograph so faded that it is hard to
make out. The urgency and tenderness of Rilke's poem
concludes rather darkly with an avowal of the poet's own

mortal presence. Ashbery's poem takes a different route; resisting any suggestion of darkness, it ends with an assertion of poetic possibility.

MIXED FEELINGS

A pleasant smell of frying sausages
Attacks the sense, along with an old, mostly invisible
Photograph of what seems to be girls lounging around
An old fighter bomber, circa 1942 vintage.
How to explain to these girls, if indeed that's what
    they are,
These Ruths, Lindas, Pats and Sheilas
About the vast change that's taken place
In the fabric of our society, altering the texture
Of all things in it? And yet
They somehow look as if they knew, except
That it's so hard to see them, it's hard to figure out
Exactly what kind of expressions they're wearing.
What are your hobbies, girls? Aw nerts,
One of them might say, this guy's too much for me.
Let's go on and out, somewhere
Through the canyons of the garment center
To a small café and have a cup of coffee.
I am not offended that these creatures (that's the word)
Of my imagination seem to hold me in such light esteem,
Pay so little heed to me. It's part of a complicated
Flirtation routine, anyhow, no doubt. But this talk of
The garment center? Surely that's California sunlight
Belaboring them and the old crate on which they
Have draped themselves, fading its Donald Duck insignia
To the extreme point of legibility.
Maybe they were lying but more likely their
Tiny intelligences cannot retain much information.
Not even one fact, perhaps. That's why
They think they're in New York. I like the way
They look and act and feel. I wonder
How they got that way, but am not going to
Waste any more time thinking about them.
I have already forgotten them
Until some day in the not too distant future
When we meet possibly in the lounge of a modern airport,
They look as astonishingly young and fresh as when this
    picture was made

But full of contradictory ideas, stupid ones as well as
Worthwhile ones, but all flooding the surface of our minds
As we babble about the sky and the weather and the
      forests of change.

So one experiences the gradual wearing away of the
already old, mostly invisible photograph of some girls
lounging around a fighter bomber in 1942. The process of
wearing away is carried on by the continual subversion
not only of the photographic image but of what it stands
for. First, the girls cannot be aware of the vast changes
that have taken place since they were photographed, so
whatever claims they might have on the present in which
they are being viewed are undermined. Their expressive-
ness can also be discounted because their faces are difficult to make out. The poet, at a loss as to how to approach
the girls, asks a silly question about what hobbies they
have. The girls want to get away from this most unhip
of voyeurs to a place that is clearly not in the photograph.
And he's not offended. Why should he be? He's the source
for whatever they do. We might consider the imagined
resistance of the girls as part of the complicated flirtation
that enables poems to be written. For how can these girls,
having no wills of their own and such tiny intelligences,
really resist? If they think they're in New York, it's because
the poet wants them there—where the poem is. And once
he has them there, far from the California climate of the
photograph, he can forget them until the possibility arises
of using them again. And when that happens, it will be
in a thoroughly poetic context, one that is not so emphati-
cally temporal as the photograph, and that will allow them
to exist with their youth and vitality restored. They will
be full of contradictory ideas, flooding the surface of their
minds and the mind of which they are a part—the poet's
mind—as they babble about the sky and the weather and
the forests of change—stock items, down to the plangency
of the final metaphor in the life of most lyric poems. So,
the best is yet to come. At least, that's what we are led to
believe. For doesn't the poem shift our attention from the
inevitable death (by fading) of the photograph to the future, which will be a poem? "Mixed Feelings" began by
looking back and ends by looking ahead. It represents a

refusal to mourn—not just the passing of four girls or the era they represent, but anything at all; it says *no* to the conventional claims of photography—that "they" (the photographic subjects) are changed or gone—that those who were young and happy are now, alas, old or dead. Its upbeat ending is not an expected response or even, many would say, an acceptable one. More and more the poem seems like a case of somebody's family photo fallen into the wrong hands.

VII

ON CHARLES WRIGHT'S POEM 'BAR GIAMACIA 1959–60': THE POEM AS PHOTOGRAPH

If Ashbery's poem acknowledges the gratuitous and arbitrary existence of an exploitable photo with the same offhandedness that it takes notice of sausages frying, only to discard it in the end, nothing of the same could possibly be said of Charles Wright's poem, "Bar Giamacia, 1959–60," which is saturated with the sort of sadness I have associated with family photographs and which draws its emotional power not by compensating for photography's limitations, but by identifying with photography's peculiar and undeniable power to touch us.

BAR GIAMACIA 1959–60

Grace is the focal point,
                    the tip ends of her loosed hair
Like match fire in the back light,
Her hands in a "Here's the church . . ."
                              She's looking at Ugo Mulas,
Who's looking at us.

Ingrid is writing this all down, and glances up, and stares
          hard.

This still isn't clear.

I'm looking at Grace, and Goldstein and Borsuk and
          Dick Venezia
Are looking at me.
                              Yola keeps reading her book.

And that leaves the rest of them: Susan and Elena and
          Carl Glass.

And Thorp and Schimmel and Jim Gates,
                    and Hobart and Schneeman
One afternoon in Milan in the late spring.

Then Ugo finishes, drinks a coffee, and everyone goes
    away.
Summer arrives, and winter;
                the snow falls and no one comes back
Ever again,
    all of them gone through the star filter of memory,
With its small gravel and metal tables and passers-by . . .

An image, a kind of family photograph, is put together
before our eyes, and despite all the looking that takes place
within the poem, nothing is clear until everyone is ac-
counted for. Then, and only then, can the season and the
place be named. The focus or clarity of the poem coincides
with the sudden inclusion of the event in time. The poem
celebrates the sad moment when we become history—
the photographic moment, the moment written about, the
moment when everyone goes away, when everyone suddenly ceases to be what they were. Of course, the world
goes about its business as it has to: seasons follow, life
goes on, the participants in the little party go their separate ways, never to reconvene, not in the world, nor in the
poet's imagination—that star filter of memory, with its
small metal tables and passers-by. The image is forlorn,
even grave, and, with the mention of passers-by, it does the
extraordinary; it enacts its own forgetability, taking a last
look at itself. But the moment of loss, which hovered at
the brink of oblivion, is saved. The poem says what most
photographs that commemorate moments say, and what
John Ashbery, in "Mixed Feelings" at least, resists saying.
That is, "They were here, you can see they were here, and
now they're gone." But beyond that, because it ends with
an ellipsis, it suggests that an empty stage, with its props
—the tables and passers-by—waits to be filled, that another reunion, another convening of elements from the
past, will take place, and another poem will be written.
The Rilke and the Ashbery poems assume the burden
of completing or continuing what was begun in a photograph. Charles Wright's poem is a slightly different case

since it never tells us that it is based on a photo. Rather, the poem constructs a photograph as it proceeds, so that it may affect us as photographs do. It even fades at the end, as if to make way for itself—the poem that it is, and the poem that it will be.

MASTERPIECES AND THE MUSEUM

Arthur C. Danto

Not long ago, I participated in a symposium on the concept of the masterpiece at a major East Coast museum which felt it would be an extremely useful thing to know what a masterpiece was. The other panelists were art historians or curators, and each was far more directly engaged with works of art than I, as a philosopher, could ever be: I accepted the invitation because I thought it would be interesting to think about the concept, the practical implications of which I hoped to learn more about from colleagues who had to decide which works of art were masterpieces, and had to justify those decisions to other scholars or to boards of trustees. What astonished me as talk followed talk that day was the clear reluctance of any of the speakers to address the topic we had been summoned to clarify. Each of them spoke of the overall degradation of the term "masterpiece" in contemporary usage, and each had a witty slide or two to establish this fact, usually from an advertisement for a prestigious automobile or a luxurious hotel, in which the reader was urged to "drive a masterpiece" or even to "spend a weekend with a masterpiece." There can be little doubt that the advertising industry has appropriated "masterpiece" to glamorize mere items of price and opulence by association with high art. But we all use the term rather casually, almost like "work of art" itself, to praise a soufflé or a salad, or a business letter or even an advertising jingle, though enough irony is carried over into these uses that it is fair to infer that the essential meaning of the term is largely intact.

Still, nearly all of the speakers proceded to lecture on a topic chosen, one felt, to be as far from the concept of masterpiece as could be found, as if they were made uncomfortable by the concept. This could have been a form of diffidence, but my colleagues were really not diffident people: each had an enviable and international reputation, and each spoke with authority. The last talk was by a militant feminist curator, whose view was that the concept is hopelessly intertwined with white male oppression; she showed work by women or by minority artists, or in some cases works that ridiculed the very idea of the masterpiece, and the implication of her talk was that the entire concept, together with the pattern of domination and privilege with which it was connected, required retirement. She seemed to propose that the task of the artist was no longer to produce masterpieces, but to make and show art for some more socially urgent endeavor. Why should making art be the way to achieve political goals that might be more effectively pursued through other avenues? Perhaps because the institutionalization of privilege is sufficiently integral to our society that to weaken it at any point is to weaken it at every point— and art of a certain aggressive form might after all be a pretty powerful weapon, given the social values embodied in works of art—masterpieces, say—and the sensitivities that would be bruised by just the kind of art she showed us that day. In a distant way, her strategy was a variant of Dada, which attacked through art the scheme of values that was held responsible for the First World War.

In any case, her talk was an abrupt reminder that the museum, like the university, has become an arena of political conflict, as more and more people who, young in the late 1960s and radicalized then, now seek to impose their agenda on the institutions they have begun to penetrate. We find in the conflict over canons, in the urgency that attaches to black studies and women's studies, the same deep transformative pressures she was implying in her mocking address. Perhaps such pressures also explain why curators and scholars, white and male and prosperous, backed away from the masterpiece. It had become a charged concept, more than a degraded one, and all the energies of our conflicted institutions of art converged upon it. Each of the panelists sought some oblique way of addressing the topic, as if each had a history of having to confront angry charges or deal with accusations of élitism, discrimination, harassment, oppression. The concept of masterpiece was not the innocent topic I had supposed it was. In fact, as I shall show, it never was an innocent concept.

The other talks were doubtless interesting. One of the scholars, for example, discussed what he rather cutely called "monsterpieces"—depictions of monsters in ancient statuary and painting. From his talk I learned, for example, some interesting facts about centaurs, gorgons, many-headed dogs, and the like. It struck me, while looking at his slides, that archaic effigies of centaurs showed them with their genitals between their forelegs, as if the centaur were a human being with an equine set of hindquarters, just as we think of mermaids as essentially human females with fishy bottoms: it would shock us to think of a mermaid as a fish, say as something we could serve poached. It occurred to me that by the Renaissance, the genitals had migrated back to the rear quarters of the centaur, in paintings of them such as Botticelli's, as if, with the upsurge of Christianity, the genitals were relegated to the beast in us, whereas the antique sculptor assumed that our humanity was implicated with our sexual identity. With the translocation of genitals in later art, the centaur does come out a far more integral creature than in archaic representations, where he seems cobbled out of disjoint bodily parts. But then—and this was a reflection connected with a topic of deep concern to me, namely the different limits of words and images— I thought that later centaurs were solutions to a problem the early ones had to solve somehow, namely how to show what is easy to describe as a creature part human and part horse. For example, the description does not tell us where the genitals are to be located, but the artist has to decide between which pair of the creature's legs they are to be situated. A scholar of my acquaintance is writing about chaos these days, and simply think of how easy it is to say, "The center cannot hold," and how difficult it would be to devise a pictorial equivalent. So it was a useful talk for my purposes, but hardly for the purposes of the conference, for the relationship between master-piece and monster-piece was never broached. Another scholar talked about the difference between the real and the fake. And another about caricatures, admittedly by artists who could or even did produce masterpieces, though the connection between the two was, by now predictably, left untouched. And then it was my turn to talk.

As usual, I had no slides to show, since mine was intended as a philosophical talk. Moreover, even when, as a critic, I write on art, I rarely am able to use pictures, and so I always seek to describe two or three works in such a way that the reader can construct the image, within limits. I have become something of a master of what the ancients called *ekphrasis*—which literally is putting pictures into words. This in fact was a form of literary exercise in ancient times, and its greatest paradigm is supposed to have been Homer's description of the Shield of Achilles. That is a great set piece of ekphrasis, but it is also something of a failure, for it is impossible to reconstruct from it any sense of what the shield really looked like. Whenever I wander through an exhibit of Greek vases, I look for one showing Thetis giving her great son the armor forged for him by Hephaestus, just to see how an ancient artist dealt with this problem. In fact they did not even try, and the usual shield is a simple round affair, leaving it to the imagination of the viewer perhaps to fill in the detail. In my view the impossibility of visualizing the shield is the best evidence we have that Homer was blind, that he really never saw an image, and so had no sense that an artist who worked in images had different limits from one who worked in words. Here I am, you might want now to say, also evading the subject. But something more central to the issue turns on the matter of slides.

I thought by the time I spoke the audience would have seen so many masterpieces that I could easily refer to someone else's slide if I needed an example. In fact we had by then seen several hundred slides, among them slides of advertisements, monsterpieces, cartoons, and any number of deliberately selected nonmasterpieces—but by my reckoning only three masterpieces had been shown altogether. In fact, I am certain, had I handed out a questionnaire, there would have been not the slightest doubt in anyone's mind which were the masterpieces, so

it is not as though any of us has any difficulty in picking
them out. There are certain works so involved in the
meaning of the term that to refuse to call them masterpieces would be as incoherent as to insist upon calling
others by that exalting term. *Rembrandt in His Studio*
would without question be counted a masterpiece, while
The Artist in His Studio by William Sidney Mount would
equally certainly not be, and in fact it might be questioned whether Mount were capable of a masterpiece,
even if a good-enough painter. So the question would not
be which are the masterpieces—we know this—but why
we have the concept and what it means that we use it.
What was *not* discussed at the symposium certainly threw
some light on these questions: the most eloquent communication made that day was the tense diffidence, the
willed silence, the diversionary and deflected inattention
to the topic of the day. The feminist curator's interven-
tion suggested that we are undergoing a moment similar
to that in which the masterpiece, as we know it, came to
dominate our concept of art—a moment of upheaval and
indeed of revolution. Both moments are connected with
transformations in the concept of the museum as an institution, and it is not surprising that the masterpiece
carries the weight of political attitude, especially when
a masterpiece of art is considered beyond politics. Part
of what we mean in calling a work of art a masterpiece is
that it is of "museum quality." And the museum itself is
a deeply contested idea in the world today.

I have heard it said that the museum and the guillotine
were invented together, and in historical truth they
do refer to one another, for it was in part works confis-
cated from those whose heads were severed in the revolutionary fervor that formed the contents of the first museum in the modern sense of the term. It was Bertrand
Barère, "*l'Anachreon de la guillotine*," who in 1791 proposed creation of a national museum in France. Jean-
Honoré Fragonard, the artist one associates most closely
with the spirit of the *ancien régime*, survived the Revolution as a proto-curator in the Louvre, just when his erstwhile patroness, to whose genius we owe Fragonard's

masterpiece, *The Progress of Love*, met her end under
the blade at the other end of the Tuileries gardens. And
Fragonard's patron, the Abbé de Saint-Non—known after
the Revolution as Citizen Vivant-Denon—became the
Director General of what came to be the Musée Napoleon, the prototype of the great museum of modern
times. Vivant-Denon was the first great curatorial im-
presario, part pirate, part artist, the model for Thomas
Hoving and, perhaps, Thomas Krens, the new director
of the Guggenheim Museum in New York. We owe to
Vivant-Denon our concepts of museum and of masterpiece. Cecil Gould, who wrote a fine study of the Musée
Napoleon, gives it three parents, an improbable pro-
genitive image but an historically correct one: repub-
licanism, anticlericalism, and a successful aggressive war.
You hardly can get more political than that, not even with
feminism, minority rights, and gay liberation.

In the eighteenth century as in antiquity, the possession of art was a symbol of authority, and the violent
seizure of someone else's art was, like raping his women,
a symbolic appropriation of his authority and the metaphorical demonstration of his impotency. Authority was,
equally symbolically, transferred to the people from their
rulers when their art was seized in the name of the Revolution. "Every citizen who entered the Louvre," according to a recent history, "inherited the collections of the
kings of France." It became the natural right of "the
people" to possess these works that had been among the
appurtenances of their subjugation. Similarly, authority
passed from the Church to the secular estate through the
forced transfer of ecclesiastical art to republican hands.
One could see these works in the same spirit in which one
could see the displayed heads of fallen aristocrats. Systematic confiscation brought so many works to the Louvre
that simply inventorying the aggregation became a heavy
labor. Fragonard was one of six members of the Commission du Musée Central, and drawing up the inventory
was one of his main tasks, bureaucratizing the fruits of
violence and rapine. The museum entered modern consciousness an emblem of power, not simply as a place to
see aesthetically impressive works, or to study the mas-

ters. There had always been that kind of access for scholars and artists, at the owners' pleasure. Here attendance
was a *right*.

Primitives ate their enemies' hearts; Napoleon seized
incredible quantities of art on his expeditions, especially
in Italy, the Lowlands, Germany, and Egypt. Initially,
this was on behalf of the Musée Central—he was ordered
by the Directoire to confiscate the most celebrated monu-
ments as a way of expressing the dominion of liberty and
equality. The French, drunk on historical analogy, saw
themselves as the inheritors of ancient Roman republi-
cans, saw, indeed, the mission of civilization as having
passed from Rome to Paris—and the forced transfer of
works of art from one to the other enacted this. Napoleon,
from what I have been able to discover, was not greatly
interested in art as such, which he simply regarded as
the imitation of nature: as he could see no interest in
imitation when he could have the originals, he saw no
point in art. But he did see the magical meaning of
artworks as trophies. In an engraving from 1810, a pro-
cession moves along the Grande galerie, with the masterpieces of world art that Napoleon had stolen accompany-
ing the march like so many crowned heads impaled on
pikes. When Napoleon was defeated, the repatriation of
artworks was a symbolic reclamation of authority by their
original owners, not a quenching of aesthetic thirst of
those who had been deprived.

There has never been quite so glorious an art collection
as that possessed in its short life by the Musée Napoléon
—which is what the Musée Central became—though one
supposes that Hitler's happily aborted Führermuseum,
acquired on the same principles, would have given it a
run for the money. Nor can we overestimate the degree
to which the modern national museum owes its form and
its existence to the Bonaparte mentality: Louis Bonaparte
founded what is now the Rijkmuseum in Amsterdam; the
Prado was initiated by Joseph Bonaparte; the Brera, in
Milan, was founded in 1803 and got its best pieces from
Eugène Beauharnais, Napoleon's stepson. But the idea
of an aggregation of masterpieces, having in common only
their museum quality, has been a dominant component

in the concepts of museum and works of art ever since;
and inasmuch as power remains as a third component,
who owns the museum remains the dividing question of
contemporary discussion. During the question period, at
the end of our symposium, a young woman wanted to
know, regarding certain works on paper by Georgia
O'Keeffe, whether they did not have a rightful place "in
the museum." I offered in response a criterion of the masterpiece: Ask yourself, if you were Napoleon, whether
you would steal those works. If not, they are not masterpieces, and belong in museums only if we change the
concept of the museum. I do not believe my questioner
quite wanted the concept changed: she wanted the museum to retain its posture of artistic authority, and if the
museum is in fact the domain of whites and males, then
to get the work of a woman hung there is to acquire a
bit of that power for women, is to achieve a political
victory. When the Lila Acheson Wallace wing of the
Metropolitan Museum was opened, it was greeted with
characteristic outrage by the irate editorialist of the conservative *New Criterion*, for whom the Metropolitan, in
his words, is "the museum of masterpieces," it being his
complaint that few of the works housed in the new wing
would, by my old criterion, have been worth stealing.
There was considerable question in the final days of the
Musée Napoleon about which works were worth keeping in the Louvre, the inferior remainder being consigned,
to provincial chagrin, to the museums of provincial
France: "provincial" remains the antonym, in the *New
Criterion* lexicon, of "masterpiece." And so, in a way, does
"political." When the Museum of Modern Art showed
some works intended as public art by Vito Acconci con-
currently with a show of politically engaged prints in an
exhibition called "Committed to Print," *New Criterion*
writers accused the museum of selling out to fashionable
radicalism, and made the ancillary claim that politics had
no place in the museum. But the museum is, to use an
expression widely borrowed from Jacques Derrida, "always already" political in its very inception. The struggle
that gave a shape to the conference on the masterpiece
was not between the political and the nonpolitical, but

between two political positions, one held so long that it had until recently been forgotten, or had suppressed the consciousness of how political it was. The diffidence of curators and scholars at the conference reflected an uncertainty about the mission of the museum today. There are many demands upon the museum, coming from quarters that it had previously excluded. The feminist curator wanted to dilute the pool of masterpieces in order to dissolve the power and intimidation they express, to weaken the concept of the museum as defined by masterpieces, making it possible for the museum to show works for which the issue of theft has no application. Museums play too important a role in contemporary culture just to be storehouses of symbolic authority, and perhaps it is necessary to defeat that storehouse function if the museum is to discharge its other duties. The insistence that museums contain only masterpieces, as well as the mocking, often abusive language of the defenders and attackers of this position, can best be understood through the opposition to an alternative view of museums.

By now, I think, it must be plain that the masterpiece has come to play a role in a strife that is at once political and conceptual. Conceptually, the question has to do with the point of art, with the politics pulling the concept in two directions. The point of placing masterpieces of classical art on trophaic display, according to an eighteenth-century figure cited by Francis Henry Taylor in his wonderful book on the history of collecting, was this: "By seeing the models of antiquity, [the French people] will train its feelings and its critical sense." The feelings at issue would not have been aesthetic so much as moral, and the critical sense would be trained in learning to explain the success with which moral meaning is expressed by formal means. The museum did not exist for pleasure or the development of taste, but for the moral education of the citizenry. And this may be confirmed by reflecting on the kind of art that would have been produced at the time of the Musée Napoleon—didactic, moralistic art, the kind approved of already by Diderot in his *Salons*, already the kind of art the Academy sought to encourage even before the Revolution, the kind of art

that put quit to Fragonard's career as painter of erotic
frivolities and kicked him upstairs as curator in the museum that celebrated artistic values antithetical to his
and his lopped erstwhile patrons. The masterpiece as an
essentially contested concept today is on the defensive
because a moral role is being asked of art other than the
one it came to play in the revolutionary era. Hitler wrote,
indeed inscribed in his *Haus der Deutsche Kunst,* that
"Art is a mission demanding fanaticism." There have
been many missions for art, all fanatically advanced, and
each connected with a different moral vision.

The moral mission for art endorsed by those who
today attack the concept of art, or who put forward
as masterpieces works everyone knows not to be masterpieces at all, is also in part an attack on two artistic ideals
central to our concept of the masterpiece, the ideals,
namely, of the Master and the Genius. The revolutionary
impulses today aim to overthrow the institution in which
these two ideal artistic types have a defining place. In
a form of artistic production where neither mastery nor
genius have a place, there can be no such thing as a
masterpiece; and the museum must be transformed if it
is no longer internally related to the concept of the masterpiece.

Let me make vivid the contrast between the Master
and the Genius—and ultimately the contrast between
the system of artistic production whose poles they determine, and that from which they have been systematically
erased—by discussing their counterparts in another culture altogether. The Minister and the Poet in classical
Chinese culture are embodied respectively in Confucius
and Lao Tzu. One can see the difference between them in
their conflicting views of language. For the Confucian, a
primary administrative task would be what Confucius,
the Master, calls "The Rectification of Names." There
was no intention of setting up a visionary calculus in
which unambiguous names were inscribed for each thing,
of the kind dreamt of by Leibniz in the seventeenth century, or by some of the Logical Positivists in our own,
but only the intention that usage be stabilized in order

that communication can be clear and direct, with as little ambiguity as possible. The French Academy, with its lexicographic obligations, might be considered to discharge this Confucian function. Lao Tzu, by contrast, begins his great philosophical poem by expressing the deepest mistrust of language as language—"The Way that can be spoken of is not the True Way." Clearly, the Master assigns a priority to uniform usage and a value to discourse which the Taoist rejects. For the Taoist, whatever use of language may be made by a poet, it would have nothing to do with the system of usages the Minister is obliged to legislate. These diverging attitudes toward language exemplify the two systems of difference generated by the two opposed ideals. For Confucius, a proper human life cannot be lived without rules, where once more it is conformity to rule that matters more than the specific rules conformed to. The entirety of Confucius's masterpiece, the *Analects*, is made up of conversations between the Master and his adherents, in which they undertake to determine what would be the right thing to do in situations not as yet covered by a rule. Ministers will after all be required—alas, the Master would sigh—to make decisions in unstructured circumstances, but when in them they must act as to imply a rule. My favorite Confucian saying is this: "If I hold up one corner and a man cannot come back to me with the other three, I do not continue the lesson." The Taoist, again by contrast, was committed to eccentricity: were he to hold up *his* corner, he would leave it a puzzle as to what his corner was a corner of, and then how many other corners there might be: the fact that Confucius already has in mind a regular rectangular form, hence an artifact like an altar cloth or a blanket—rather than an animal skin or a pile of leaves—yields by itself an insight into his vision of an ordered world and a practical system of knowledge. The Taoist did not see the world composed of neat four-cornered practical bits, but instead made up of irregular things that sought not to conform to our needs and wants, but to the Way. Taoists admire trees that grow large and last a long time because they cannot be pressed into human needs except as yielding Taoist metaphors: "If you try to judge it by conventional standards, you will be way off," an enlightened Taoist carpenter says, where the Confucian carpenter is defined by straight edge and plumb bob and right angle. Taoist calligraphy conceals; Taoist poetry is paradoxical: each brings enlightenment by shunning what the Confucian deemed central.

I do not know when the concept of genius first entered our Western conception of artistic creativity, though the contrast between artist and craftsman is already present in the dialogue *Ion*, by Plato, where Socrates maliciously explains that Ion has a great gift as a rhapsode and can move men's minds, but lacks knowledge and so depends upon inspiration. The craftsman is the Socratic paradigm of he who has knowledge. Ion cannot teach, cannot pass on to others what he has but inherited; the craftsman is the model of the teacher. Socrates' carpenters and cobblers get to be the Master in our tradition, while Ion, possessed and driven by forces outside and higher than himself, gets to be the Genius. But I do not think the Genius gets to be conceptually important, despite eccentrics like Piero di Cosimo, until the high Renaissance and Michelangelo.

It is one thing to set up the two ideals, as the Confucian and the Taoist: it is another to imagine what it would be like to have to be both. The two ideals collide in an artist like Albrecht Durer. Durer's background was precisely that in which artistic preeminence was defined through attaining mastery, and hence to be a master, the head of a workshop, the producer of work to order, like a tailor of customized costumes, one who had internalized the rules and adhered to them as a condition of practicing an art that really was not discriminated from a craft. But Durer was powerfully drawn to another ideal, as embodied in Michelangelo, whose illuminating myth, to my mind, was his ambition of carving the entire marble quarry at Carrara into some vast colossus, or who singlehandedly executed the program of the Sistine ceiling. It little mattered that he had helpers—we are dealing not with art, historical truth, but with art, historical myth. A Master who did not have helpers would not be a Master, but it belongs to the myth that Michelangelo should have confronted that vast vault on his own, and with his own hands laid down every patch of paint, producing a work beyond emulation, for which rules could not be found: it was a work that belonged to The Sublime, which is the habitat of Genius. Panofsky writes about Durer's difficult and unhappy marriage (while Masters marry, Genius is lonely). The problem in part was due to the fact that he took as wife a woman who had been brought up to be *Frau Meister*, but who could not adjust to the conflicting demands of being the companion of Genius. We admire Michelangelo for his wild abundance, his readiness to break rules, placing volutes, for example, on the floor of the Laurentian Library and enlarging them.

The concept of the Master presupposes a certain institutional reality. One ascends to Masterhood through stages, and by presenting a masterpiece to prove one's mastery. There is an implicit educational institution, the rules of which are well defined, and one's acceptance of the rules is the precondition for entering the system and emerging as Master. This system may be less to protect the public, according to Arnold Hauser, the social historian of art, than to protect the artist from interference from the public, by controlling competition, entry into the craft, and the like: the length of the work day, wages, the period of apprenticeship, the requirements of the masterpiece. This system lives on in the graduate system of education in the United States, where the dissertation is the prescribed masterpiece. Rarely is a dissertation, in any further than the licensing sense, a masterpiece— it is supposed to be "a contribution to knowledge." Bergson's doctoral dissertation satisfied the conditions for the graduate-student masterpiece, but also showed the originality we demand in a masterpiece in that further sense. And Wittgenstein's *Tractatus* is an unusual doctoral dissertation, though in fact he became a doctor by defending it successfully in front of Bertrand Russell and G. E. Moore. It happens to be one of the great philosophical works of the century, but it is hardly the model for a dissertation, or there would be far too few doctors of philosophy for the educational system. Who would require "something like the Sistine ceiling" for the Master of Fine Arts degree? The degree would simply disappear. As the work that defines being a Master, the masterpiece would have to be the kind of work a reasonably instructed person can achieve if sufficiently industrious. I would be astonished if the typical degree-granting philosophy department would accept as a dissertation something like the *Tractatus*: the candidate would be hounded by demands to clarify and explain to which, as a genius, Wittgenstein was regarded immune. You cannot institutionalize the Genius, and if the Genius enters into our concept of art, neither can you institutionalize that.

The history of art, if artists were only thought of as masters, would be like the history of some technology— a history of progress over design and function, with breakthroughs of various sorts, then long periods of simple practice.

To confront the concept of genius directly, I perhaps can not do better than cite Kant, in whose writings on art the genius figures prominently and, one might say, romantically:

> Everyone is agreed that genius is opposed to the spirit of imitation. Now since learning is nothing but imitation, it follows that the greatest ability and teachability qua teachability cannot avail for genius. Even if a man thinks or invents for himself, and does not merely take in what others have taught, even if he discovers many things in art and science, this is not the right ground for calling such a (perhaps great) head a genius . . . for even these things could be learned. They lie in the natural path of him who investigates and reflects according to the rules; and they do not differ specifically from what can be acquired by industry through imitation.

There is a special kind of originality in genius, on this formulation, in that even if one has not learned to do what one does, it is not an exercise of genius if it could have been learned. The first person to make ice cream was original, but ice cream is no different in taste if produced by someone who learned how from an ice-cream master. It is perhaps for this reason that originality of the learnable order has to be protected: it does not matter to the product who was first. So we have copyrights and patents and licenses and closely guarded secrets that we divulge only for a fee or as a franchise, which can in principle be stolen. Hence the Master requires a further institutionalization for infringements. Picasso wittily said he was a rich man because he had sold the license for painting guitars, and in truth painting guitars was something anyone could do, it was deeply imitable, though the gift of Picasso's originality was not. An institution gives the Master an exclusive right to a certain product, but the product is not inferior if the secret is stolen: originality does not register on the tongue, and if you have found out the secret of cooking blackened redfish, the legend "the original home of blackened redfish" on the menu of origin is mere advertisement.

There are plenty of problems in getting the distinction between Genius and Master to stick, but the difference might be thought parallel to that in which taste is contrasted with following rules. For taste is something that functions in the abeyance of rules, and rules are there precisely for those who do not possess taste. There are many moral qualities for which something like this is true: a kind person is so through his or her character, not through following certain rules; a considerate person is one who knows what to do in cases where there are no rules. There was a formal regulation enacted in Nuremburg in 1596 which required painters to produce a masterpiece by a certain time—much as we require doctoral candidates to complete the dissertation at the end of seven years. But if we connect the masterpiece with genius in such a way that only a genius can produce a masterpiece, how is such legislation possible? Surely, since Kant, we have established something like this connection, moving the concept of the masterpiece away from the concept of the master, complicating it by requiring that its maker be master and genius at once.

The state can legislate the production of masterpieces, as for instance with the rules governing standards for the precisely designated *doctorat d'état* of the French academic system—but it cannot require those who produce them to be geniuses. It may be for just this reason that works of genius have to be stolen by the Napoleons of the world, or bought for fortunes, since they cannot, so to speak, be grown in the academies and schools the Napoleons can set up for training people to make porcelains and tapestries and the like. The work of genius, as inherently original and unique, connects the Napoleon-style museum with the older *Wunderkammer*, containing objects of rarity and power that could not be the production of an industry. This raises a difficult question for art education which, on the one hand, must culminate in a body of masterwork as a condition of certification, but which, if merely that, falls short of art in its highest sense as calling for genius. That works of genius cannot be the products of an industry raises serious questions as well for public art, where the state is asked to forfeit its own criteria in favor of the free imperative of the artistic genius, which any artist good enough to be commissioned is supposed to have a touch of. The masterpiece was always a complex matter of negotiation between patron and painter, the former insisting on just what he wanted, the latter defining his rights against that. But genius has come to demand a complete freedom in return for which we expect—a masterpiece, a work of absolute originality. But why, since the entry of this concept into the structure in which Master and Patron understood one another so naturally, should there be this forfeiture of regulation? What is it that the masterpiece, now understood as a work into which genius flows, is supposed to yield as the price of absolute artistic freedom? Kant writes, again obscurely but with great power, as follows:

> Genius is the talent (or natural gift) which gives the rule to art. Since talent, as the innate productive faculty of the artist, belongs itself to Nature, we may express the matter thus: Genius is the innate mental disposition through which Nature gives the rule to art.

This fuses, whatever the cost in individual psychology, the impulses of Confucian and Taoist into one. The Genius is a kind of legislator, giving a rule. So others can follow that rule, without themselves having to be geniuses. But the rule comes from Nature through the Genius, as the medium of Nature, and because it is from Nature, the rule is more than a rule: it is a law, and, as a law, universal. It is this universality, I think, under which the work of genius addresses humankind as humankind, which then marks the masterpiece in modern usage, even if we are uncomfortable with its Kantian premises. The masterpiece is a work for all, not just its patron, not just for its time and place. It is meant as timeless, it is supposed to transcend its historical moment. We flock to the Sistine Chapel not to be informed as to the values of the sixteenth-century popes. We go to be touched in our essential universal humanity.

The critic Robert Hughes declares Lucian Freud's *Large Interior, W.11 (After Watteau)* of 1981–83 "perhaps his own masterpiece, at least in terms of size and pictorial ambition." The expression "his own masterpiece" strikes a strange note, though an exact one here, in connection with this artist whose self appears a component in all his work and not merely in his chilling self-portraits. And the qualifying "at least" is appropriate as well: size, and pictorial ambition, go with being a masterpiece: in satisfying these conditions, Freud met the conditions of the masterpiece within the limits of his powers. Obviously, there are small masterpieces, and size perhaps refers to something like greatness, metaphorically (Napoleon was a tiny man). The Master undertook to show, in the masterpiece, what he was capable of, so "size" takes on a further metaphorical connotation of arduousness and difficulty of execution, of something only a master could bring off. One feels it is not a masterpiece if it is not difficult or if, as the expression goes, "anyone could do that." This canvas of Lucian Freud's refers to and transforms the painting *Pierrot content* of Watteau, which though a wonderful painting is not one of Watteau's masterpieces. Watteau's masterpieces are the *Embarkation for Cythera* and, of course, *The Shopsign of Gersaint*. Both of these have scale and pictorial ambition, but in addition each touches something of the greatest human depth. It must have been painting of this depth that Hegel had in mind when he claimed that art gives sensuous embodiment to the Idea, and hence belongs with philosophy and religion as modes of Absolute Spirit. Watteau's masterpieces concern the responsibilities of love and the transformations of time and the facing of change and death, and each is an occasion for meditations of the most oceanic order. They express the meaning of life. I do not know that Lucian Freud is capable of that level of achievement, which may be why Hughes, who admires Freud greatly and thinks him our greatest realist painter, nevertheless speaks of this work as "Perhaps his own masterpiece." It is a haunting painting, but for reasons I cannot pause to ponder, it is a glacial one, and it remains, as Freud's work always does, a complex and essentially sexual transaction between the artist's will and the submission to it of reluctant models: his figures look tense, strained, posed, uncomfortable: they look the way we feel when we contemplate these sadistic works. They are about domination, and though perhaps this is a masterpiece of perversion, a true masterpiece is not a "masterpiece of" (any more than it is someone's own)—and since most of the uses of the term "masterpiece" in common use are "masterpieces of"—of engineering, of luxury—the term perhaps is not quite so degraded as my fellow panelists insisted.

This suggests to me a further point: that an artist's masterpiece and the body of the master's work must refer to one another in a certain way, so that someone could not produce a masterpiece whose work did not already possess a certain kind of philosophical depth. At his most frivolous, there is an underside of metaphysical intention in Watteau. *Las Meninas* is a masterpiece by the criteria of pictorial ambition and scale, but it coheres sufficiently with anything Velázquez painted that we can see inscribed in even his lesser works the masterpiece that moves us to reflect on the reality of things. In brief, it is as if the masterpiece today is finally perceived as a work that can be produced only by a genius, so that we can, as it were, go through an artist's work and say something like this—"Though he produced no masterpieces, he could have done." The reverse is also true: seeing a work whose scale and ambition would class it as a masterpiece but where in truth it is only big and busy, we may begin to see the whole of that artist's work as somehow limited. There is an immense and foolish work by Robert Rauschenberg in the Wallace Wing of the Met that is so bad that I am no longer capable of thinking as well as I once did of his less willful work. The recent work of Jasper Johns—*The Seasons*—may be Johns's "own masterpiece" but not, I think, a masterpiece, being mainly about him: its limitations make salient this artist's limitations everywhere else, whatever auction prices may say. I adore Diebenkorn, but I think Motherwell the greater artist because the greatest of the Spanish Elegies are masterpieces and Diebenkorn has limited himself to the production of merely great paintings. There is a daring of the elements in Walter Di Maria's *Lightning Field* that redeems its scale and its vast ambition, and which dignifies everything this artist did. I oddly have the same view of Richard Serra's *Tilted Arc* whose removal from Federal Plaza in New York City I openly advocated, largely because, in my view, the masterpiece must express humanity and a work of public art instead must express the public it embodies. But Serra's piece defied the human condition of those it was imposed upon and thwarted the very values it should celebrate if a masterpiece, so its placement was incoherent with the universality.

It is easy to see why the masterpiece should be perceived as politically dangerous, especially if we are claiming rights for art produced by groups and classes which are not geniuses. Genius itself is perceived as a politically disabling category. Nonetheless, the masterpiece is a viable and even necessary concept because there is something to art beyond what bodies of rules and contractual relationships and standards of the guild can specify. It is perhaps appropriate that we should owe the concept finally to Napoleon. The scale and political ambition of his conquests were unmatched since ancient times. But they were undertaken, and in large measure succeeded, through his being bearer to the world of the great human values of the Revolution: Liberty, Equality, Fraternity. He promised something that only work as difficult and ambitious as his could achieve, and he must have seen in art, in the highest exemplifications, a mirror for his own moral grandeur.

THE MOUTH REFUSES TO TRANSLATE

Askold Melnyczuk

> I think: *serce moyeh*—
> but what I say
> my pen won't put
> on paper in
>
> this hostile tongue—
> this Jacob's ladder
> I am testing
> rung by rung.

THE TRUE SUBJECT
THE POETRY OF FAIZ AHMED FAIZ

Agha Shahid Ali

On April 5, 1988—at the height of the *intifada* in the occupied territories—a "Special to the New York Times" appeared in the paper with the headline PALESTINIAN'S POEM UNNERVES ISRAELIS. The reference was to "Those Who Pass Between Fleeting Words," by Mahmoud Darwish, probably the most popular poet in the Arab world (he also takes care of cultural affairs for the executive committee of the Palestine Liberation Organization). As usual, the focus remained on the reactions of the Israelis, their "fears." Such a syntax—which hides the very significance of the information it is giving—doesn't allow the reader to become curious, to wonder about Darwish and his poetry. How many poetry editors, after reading the *Times* story, have solicited translations of the poet? Such a syntax, by keeping the focus on the Israelis, doesn't allow one to ask: So the Palestinians, those *terrorists*, have poets? And find time, in the midst of oppression, to write *poetry*? And the PLO has a department of *cultural* affairs? The *New York Times* is not interested in the culture of the Palestinians nor, really, in that of any of the Arabic-speaking peoples. Nor is much of the United States. Professors and students in the country's Master of Fine Arts writing programs have read the Israeli poet Yehuda Amichai, but who has heard of Darwish or any other Arab poet? (Some mystically inclined ones know of the nonthreatening Kahlil Gibran.) What is particularly distressing is that despite the attention paid to the Middle East, hardly any American poet has shown curiosity about non-Israeli writers in the region (I did recently learn that W. S. Merwin is translating some Arabic poetry, including that of Darwish). Hardly any American poet has had the desire, it seems, to read between the often subversively ethnocentric lines of reports sent by American journalists in the Middle East. Why can't they see through the mystification of politics that governs those reports?

[*129*]

This ethnocentrism is not just visible in attitudes towards the Middle East; it is visible, quite clearly, in attitudes towards the entire Muslim world—a fact that may help explain why *The True Subject* (Princeton University Press, 1988), Naomi Lazard's excellent translations of Faiz Ahmed Faiz's poetry, has been virtually ignored. A handsome bilingual edition (the Urdu calligraphy by Ashfaq Ahmed is truly elegant), *The True Subject* is part of Princeton University Press's prestigious Lockert Library of Poetry in Translation series (Cavafy too is part of the series, as is Seferis), but just about no review has appeared. Why?

Curiosity about Faiz, actually, should have grown even before the appearance of these translations. In the September 1984 issue of *Harper's* (two months before Faiz died in Lahore), Edward Said, in his essay "The Mind of Winter: Reflections on Life in Exile," wrote:

> To see a poet in exile—as opposed to reading the poetry of exile—is to see exile's antinomies embodied and endured. Several years ago I spent some time with Faiz Ahmed Faiz, the greatest of contemporary Urdu poets. He had been exiled from his native Pakistan by Zia ul-Haq's military regime and had found a welcome of sorts in the ruins of Beirut. His closest friends were Palestinian, but I sensed that although there was an affinity of spirit between them, nothing quite matched—language, poetic convention, life history. Only once, when Eqbal Ahmad, a Pakistani friend and fellow exile, came to Beirut, did Faiz seem to overcome the estrangement written all over his face.

The three of them, late one night,

> sat in a dingy restaurant . . . and Faiz recited poems to us. After a time he and Eqbal stopped translating his verses for my benefit, but it did not matter. For what I watched required no translation: an enactment of homecoming steeped in defiance and loss, as if to say exultantly to Zia, "We are here."

Shouldn't these words of a truly distinguished literary critic, published in *Harper's*, a magazine rather difficult to ignore, have raised some curiosity? *Harper's* itself should have solicited translations of Faiz.*

When I came to the United States over ten years ago, I found myself frustrated at discovering that no one, absolutely no one, had heard of Faiz (at that time, very few had heard even of the Turkish poet Nazim Hikmet—a friend of Faiz's and like him a winner of the Lenin Prize for Literature; some of Hikmet's poems were translated into Urdu by Faiz). To have to introduce Faiz's name, a name that is mentioned in Pakistan—to quote Naomi Shihab Nye—as often as the sun is, seemed a terrible insult. In the subcontinent we consider him a giant. As Naomi Lazard says in her introduction to *The True Subject*, "This century has given us a few great poets whose stance and influence have altered the consciousness of the world: Pablo Neruda, César Vallejo and Ernesto Cardenal in the Western hemisphere; Nazim Hikmet and Yannis Ritsos in the Middle East; and Faiz Ahmed Faiz in South Asia." Nevertheless, one fellowship-awarding committee told Naomi Lazard that it was not convinced of the literary importance of her translation project—*this* about a poet who drew as many as fifty thousand people to his readings, a poet whose work is quoted by heart by the literate and the illiterate, a poet whose lines were recited even by those who opposed him. When UNESCO was approaching various governments to nominate *the* representative writers of their countries—for the purpose of translating them into English—the then President of Pakistan, Ayub Khan, first mentioned Faiz (and Ayub Khan, I believe, had briefly jailed him). As Edward Said says elsewhere,

> The crucial thing to understand about Faiz . . . is that like Garcia Marquez he was read and listened to both by the literary élite and by the masses. His major—indeed it is unique in any language—achievement was to have created a contrapuntal rhetoric and rhythm whereby he would

* Another poet worth bringing to America's attention is the Iranian Said Sultanpour, who was tortured during the Shah's time and executed during Khomeini's. His body was thrown into an unmarked grave.

use classical forms (*qasida, ghazal, masnavi, qita*) and transform them before his readers rather than break from the old forms. You could hear old and new together. His purity and precision were astonishing, and you must imagine therefore a poet whose poetry combined the sensuousness of Yeats with the power of Neruda. He was, I think, one of the greatest poets of this century, and was honored as such throughout the major part of Asia and Africa.

So here was this poet whose work I had grown up reciting and hearing recited by heart, a poet whose *ghazals*, lyric poems, had been (and continue to be) sung by the leading singers of the subcontinent (including the legendary Begum Akhtar), a poet who was such a master of the *ghazal* that he transformed its every stock image and, as if by magic, brought absolutely new associations into being. (For example, the beloved—an archetypal figure in Urdu poetry—can mean friend, woman, God. Faiz not only tapped into these meanings but extended them to include the Revolution. So the reader does, to quote Said, "hear old and new together." Waiting for the Revolution can be as agonizing and intoxicating as waiting for one's lover.) And yet here was a poet who was just not known in this part of the world. So I began attempting some translations, imbibing a few of the methods Adrienne Rich and W. S. Merwin had adopted in translating Ghalib, whom Faiz often echoed, but my attempts were somewhat feeble, my results uneven.

And then, quite by chance, I came across five of Naomi Lazard's translations in *Kayak*. I was immediately struck by how good they were, and I was eager to find more of her translations. I also wanted to find out more about her. Because the world—at least of poetry—can be delightfully small, a series of coincidences led me several months later to a phone conversation with her and, shortly after that, a meeting in New York. I learned that she and Carolyn Kizer were collaborating on a joint volume of Faiz translations, that Kizer had known Faiz since the 1960s, when she met him in Pakistan, and that Lazard had met him at an international literary conference in Honolulu in 1979—the only time, I believe, he was allowed into the country. Otherwise, the McCarran-Walter Act had kept him from these shores. On meeting him, Lazard says, she immediately knew she was in the presence of a poet of world stature, one who must be brought to the attention of her compatriots. And so the translation process began, right there at the conference. Lazard writes:

> We established a procedure immediately. Faiz gave me the literal translation of a poem. I wrote it down just as he dictated it. Then the real work began. I asked him questions regarding the text. Why did he choose just that phrase, that word, that image, that metaphor? What did it mean to him? There were cultural differences. What was crystal clear to an Urdu-speaking reader meant nothing at all to an American. I had to know the meaning of every nuance in order to re-create the poem.

This translation process continued across continents, through the mail; on a few occasions Lazard was able to meet Faiz during his visits to London. When Faiz died, she already had enough poems for a book; Carolyn Kizer suggested that they abandon their collaboration and that Naomi bring out her translations as a separate volume. And Princeton, luckily, proved to be an enlightened press.

In choosing the title, Lazard has shown the same care that she has exhibited throughout her project, engaged as she has been in what she calls a labor of love and conviction. By way of an epigraph, she offers a "ring of quotations regarding the true subject of poetry":

> Faiz Ahmed Faiz to Alun Lewis, Burma, circa 1943:
> "The true subject of poetry is the loss of the beloved."

> Alun Lewis, in a letter to Robert Graves
> before Lewis was killed, Burma, 1944:
> "The single poetic theme of Life and Death—the question
> of what survives of the beloved."

> Robert Graves, in *The White Goddess*,
> quoting Alun Lewis, 1947:
> "The single poetic theme of Life and Death—the question
> of what survives of the beloved."

> Naomi Lazard to Faiz Ahmed Faiz, Honolulu, 1979
> (having read *The White Goddess* many years before
> and misquoting
> the line attributed to Alun Lewis):
> "The true subject of poetry is the loss of the beloved."

And the loss of the beloved *is* the subject of Faiz's poetry,
a fact that is quite apparent in the poems included in *The
True Subject*. For example, one of the first poems Faiz
gave Lazard was "Spring Comes," the literal version of
which has the following sentence: "The book returns re-
plete with the heart's suffering"—the only time "the book"
is mentioned in the original Urdu. After learning from
Faiz that the book is a ledger in which experience is recorded, Lazard was able to give her translation its final
shape by making the book, without even mentioning it, a
controlling image:

> Spring comes; suddenly all those days return,
> all the youthful days that died on your lips,
> that have been waiting in Limbo, are born again
> each time the roses display themselves.
> Their scent belongs to you; it is your perfume.
> The roses are also the blood of your lovers.
> All the torments return, melancholy with the suffering
>   of friends,
> intoxicated with embraces of moon-bodied beauties.
> All the chapters of the heart's oppression return,
> all the questions and all the answers
> between you and me.
> Spring comes, ready with all the old accounts reopened.

Thus Spring comes—but without the beloved; as a result,
the heart continues to suffer oppression. The beloved has
the power to end this oppression, as does the Revolution
to end another kind of oppression.

In Faiz's poetry, suffering is seldom, perhaps never,
private (in the sense the suffering of confessional poets is).
Though deeply personal, it is almost never isolated from
a sense of history and injustice. In a very famous poem,
"Don't Ask Me Now, Beloved," Faiz breaks from Urdu's
traditional way of looking at the beloved. Not only does he
refuse to despair but, in a radical departure from convention, asks the beloved—even while acknowledging her
immense importance—to accept his social commitment as
more important than their love:

> Don't ask me now, Beloved, to love you as I did
> when I believed life owed its luster to your existence.
> The torments of the world meant nothing;

you alone could make me suffer.
Your beauty guaranteed the spring,
    ordained its enduring green.
Your eyes were all there was of value anywhere.
If I could have you, fate would bow before me.

None of this was real; it was all invented by desire.
The world knows how to deal out pain, apart from passion,
and manna for the heart, beyond the realm of love.
Warp and woof, the trappings of the rich are woven
by the brutish spell cast over all the ages;
human bodies numbed by filth, deformed by injuries,
cheap merchandise on sale in every street.
I must attend to this too: what can be done?
Your beauty still delights me, but what can I do?
The world knows how to deal out pain, apart from passion,
and manna for the heart, beyond the realm of love.
Don't ask from me, Beloved, love like that one long ago.

This was a revolutionary poem in Urdu, one envied by
many Urdu poets who wish they had first broken from the
tradition in which everything was either the beloved or
nothing. Faiz did not discard the tradition: the poem
clearly establishes the importance of the beloved and her
beauty. But it does some plain speaking (almost like Cor-
delia to Lear), granting love its due but no more. Of course,
that Faiz had emphasized political commitment here did
not mean that he would not, in other poems, address the
beloved in the traditional manner, showing how the speaker's life depended entirely on her. But then often, when
he is addressing the beloved, he is also addressing a figure
that, depending on the context, may very well be the
Revolution—Revolution as a lost lover or a cruel lover
who is refusing to return. So the subject of poetry continues to be true: the loss of the beloved. Even in "Don't
Ask Me Now, Beloved," the discerning reader will notice.
For that beloved, whom he was able to love exclusively
earlier, at the expense of everything else, is still beautiful,
a fact that must be acknowledged even though she does
not occupy the position she had before. The poet, thus,
accepts his political responsibilities but with an intense
awareness of the ease that has been lost. In a better world,
Faiz might be saying, he would be giving his attention
exclusively to the beloved.

In this poem, Faiz is of course drawing a line of demar-
cation between the political and the romantic. But, often,
a mingling of the political and the romantic pervades his
poetry. Sometimes the two, especially in the *ghazals*, are
entangled in such a way that there is no point in trying to
separate them: the political meaning informs the romantic
and the romantic, the political. However, Faiz, a man who
was jailed for his beliefs, obviously does have poems,
many in fact, that are exclusively political. Three such
poems appeared in *Grand Street* (Summer 1985): "Once
Again the Mind," "If You Look at the City from Here,"
and "*You* Tell Us What to Do." Each is informed by a kind
of political despair. In others, such as "The Tyrant," the
despair turns into a controlled but still passionate anger
("The Tyrant" was quoted from by Salman Rushdie in
The Nation in a piece called "Zia Unmourned." If writers
from the subcontinent, especially someone as astute as
Rushdie, are already quoting Lazard's translations to
make their points about events in that region, then hers
may very well be considered the standard translations in
English). "The Tyrant" is quite direct in its strategy:

Mine is the new religion, the new morality.
Mine are the new laws, and a new dogma.
From now on the priests in God's temple
will touch their lips to the hands of idols.
Proud men, tall as cypress trees, will bend
to lick the dwarves' feet, and taste the clay.

On this day all over earth the door
of beneficent deeds is bolted.
Every gate of prayer throughout heaven
is slammed shut today.

However, Faiz has still other political poems that are not
direct in this manner; instead, they are richly symbolic.
And the fact that they are symbolic is sometimes in itself
a political statement. Certainly, Urdu has a long enough
tradition of concealing politics in symbols. In nineteenth-
century Urdu poetry, the stock figure of the executioner
often represented the British (a way of dodging the censors
as well as the gallows: in the summer of 1857, the British
had hanged almost thirty thousand people from the trees

of Delhi to terrorize the population and punish it for what is often called the Mutiny). Naomi Lazard notes in her introduction that in Pakistan, under the censorship of the various dictatorships (including Zia's), it was "impossible to call things by their right names." Faiz's "When Autumn Came," for example, must "be read as a political poem." Despite—perhaps because of—its use of symbols, any reader or listener of Urdu would immediately grasp it as political. It focuses on the impossibility of calling things by their right names by creating a startling image: the "birds of dreams" lose their songs and thus become strangers (in the sense of exiles) to their songs. Lazard's effective translation comes up with a brilliant approximation:

> This is the way that autumn came to the trees:
> it stripped them down to the skin,
> left their ebony bodies naked.
> It shook out their hearts, the yellow leaves,
> scattered them over the ground.
> Anyone at all could trample them out of shape
> undisturbed by a single moan of protest.
>
> The birds that herald dreams
> were exiled from their song,
> each voice torn out of its throat.
> They dropped into the dust
> even before the hunter strung his bow.
>
> Oh, God of May, have mercy.
> Bless these withered bodies
> with the passion of your resurrection;
> make their dead veins flow with blood.
>
> Give some tree the gift of green again.
> Let one bird sing.

The last poem in the volume, "The Day Death Comes," recalls—quite appropriately—the beloved:

> No matter when death comes, or how,
> even though in the guise of the disdainful beloved
>   who is always cold,
> there will be the same words of farewell to the heart:
> "Thank God it is finished, the night of the broken-hearted.

Praise be to the meeting of lips,
the honeyed lips I have known."

I invite readers to discover, as Naomi Lazard has, the true subject of poetry: in a voice they have not known. Then perhaps they will grasp why Faiz Ahmed Faiz's death, on November 20, 1984, was front-page news in the papers of India, Bangladesh, the Middle East, the Soviet Union, and many other countries. The leading obituary in the *Times of London* was that of Faiz. In Pakistan, his death was the main headline in all the national dailies. Messages of condolence poured in from all over the world—from, among others, Rajiv Gandhi, Yasir Arafat, Mahmoud Darwish. A wreath was placed on his body by the Soviet ambassador to Pakistan. Even Zia ul-Haq expressed "grief." But there was not a word in the *New York Times*. And none in *Newsweek*. None in *Time*. Strangely enough, there was a brief mention in *The San Francisco Chronicle*. But the rest was silence. Naomi Lazard has done brave and lonely work.

THREE POEMS

Faiz Ahmed Faiz

GHAZAL

The heart a desecrated temple
   in it all statues of you broken
Those forgotten sorrows
   my memories of you return
   gods abandoned by their worshippers

One by one by one
   the stars light up the sky
In step with them
   you approach me in the dark
   your final destination

Tonight increase the pace
   with which the liquor is poured
   Oh tell the drummer to play a breathless beat
Worshippers have abandoned the mosques
   they're coming here to the wine house

It is the night of waiting
   tell her let no more time elapse
This pain of longing may dull
   already my memory is beginning to blur
   at any moment I may forget her

WASH THE BLOOD OFF YOUR FEET

What could I have done, gone where?
My feet were bare
and every road was covered with thorns—
of ruined friendships, of loves left behind,
of eras of loyalty that finished, one by one.

Wherever I went, in whatever direction,
my feet were soaked—
there was so much blood
that bystanders couldn't help asking:
What fashion is this, what new tradition?
For what unknown festival have you dyed your feet?

I said nothing, but they went on asking:
Why, still for nothing, are you
complaining of the utter famine of love?
There's no chance for fidelity now.

So wash this blood off your feet, they said.
Let your feet heal.
These roads, now soft with blood, will harden again.
And a hundred new paths will break through their dried **mud**.
Keep your feet ready for those roads, they said.

And be careful, they said, take care of the heart.
It still has to break,
break open into a thousand different wounds.
It still has to know knife after knife after knife.

NO TRACE OF BLOOD

There's no sign of blood, not anywhere.
I've searched everywhere.
The executioner's hands are clean, his nails transparent.
The sleeves of each assassin are spotless.
No sign anywhere: no trace of red, not
on the edge of the knife, none on the point of the sword.
The ground is without stains, the ceiling is white.
There's no sign of blood, not anywhere.

This blood which has disappeared without leaving a trace
is not part of written history:
It wasn't spilled in service of emperors,
it wasn't offered in rituals of sacrifice,
it wasn't shed in battle.
It earned no reward, had no wish granted.
No god blessed it. It was no martyr's blood.
It wasn't calligraphed on banners of victory.

But, unheard, it still kept crying out to be heard,
this orphan blood of the helpless.
No one had the time to listen, no one the desire.
It kept crying out,
but there was no witness, there was no evidence.
No case was filed.
This blood of the insignificant—from the beginning the gift of dust—
had been nourished only by dust.
In the end, still crying, it hid itself in dust.

Translated from Urdu by Agha Shahid Ali

DISAPPEARED

Dorothy Gallagher

> *Where is Juliet Stuart Poyntz?*
> *Gone. Gone with the wind.*
> Col. Bykov of the KGB to
> Whittaker Chambers.

The most pertinent facts about the disappearance of Juliet Stuart Poyntz are beyond reach, in Moscow, in the archives of whichever Soviet intelligence agency employed Poyntz during the last years of her life; also in that city, the Communist Party of the United States has long been accustomed to storing its files, and material relating to Poyntz's fate may be contained in those papers. Nevertheless, enough stray information exists to put together a plausible version of the events in which Poyntz figured more than fifty years ago.*

Our story begins on May 28, 1936. On that day, a woman who calls herself Mary Delmar goes to Chicago's Pennsylvania Station and buys a lower-berth ticket to New York. We know that Mary Delmar boards her train. Once aboard, she puts on pajamas, red pajamas as it happens. Presumably she lies down on her berth. And, presumably, as the wheels chug and the whistle blows and the lights of towns flash by, Mary Delmar thinks troubled thoughts. Then, somewhere along the line, she makes a decision: when the train stops to take on coal at Denholm, Pennsylvania, Mary Delmar, still wearing her red pajamas, jumps off. She leaves her suitcase behind, taking with her only a silver pocket knife with what seems to be a man's name crudely scratched on it; also she takes a photograph of a little boy.

---

* I am very grateful to Professor Harvey Klehr of Emory University for sending me his copy of Poyntz's FBI file, which is the source of much of the information here. Material on Poyntz's early career may be found in Theodore Draper's books on American Communism.

Whittaker Chambers's *Witness*, and Allen Weinstein's *Perjury* also deal with the Poyntz case, as does my own book, *All the Right Enemies: The Life and Murder of Carlo Tresca.*

The woman walks or runs some unspecified distance from the railroad tracks and, at last, comes to rest in a clump of bushes at the edge of a horse pasture. There, at five o'clock on the morning of May 29, she is discovered by a farmhand. He takes her to the house of his employers, a farm family named Dolan, who give her shelter.

For almost two weeks Mary Delmar remains with the Dolans. In exchange for her room and board, she is given chores to perform in the house and garden. At the end of that time Mary Delmar finds farmer Dolan's .22-caliber revolver and, on June 13, she ties her legs together with black ribbon, places a bunch of flowers between her feet, and shoots herself in the right temple.

Mary Delmar does not die. She is taken to the Lewistown Hospital where—except for a damaged eye and possible memory loss—she recovers from her wound. Prevailing opinion among the hospital staff is that she is a mental case, but one Dr. Brown is not sure. "She answers questions very well," he reports, "until you come to the point where you begin to question her concerning her past life, when she immediately develops a headache and does not recollect." Dr. Brown believes that "she has some connection that she does not wish to divulge," and that she may be "communistic," as she has no use for the rich.

If not actually crazy, Mary Delmar is surely mentally unstable at this point in her life, but she is also trying to hide her past. It will develop that her real name is Rywka Brokowicz. She will be released from the hospital into the custody of Amy MacMaster, a woman to whom she was previously unknown. Amy MacMaster will turn out to be acting on behalf of her friend Juliet Stuart Poyntz—who is the main subject of this story—and the FBI suspects (though we must always be cautious with FBI suspicions) that Delmar, or Brokowicz as we will now call her, is identical with a woman the FBI knows as "Lena" and believes to be the Soviet espionage superior of Juliet Poyntz.

Rywka Brokowicz will soon drop out of this tale, but let us follow her as far as possible. At Poyntz's request, and for a payment of twenty-five dollars a week, Amy MacMaster takes charge of Brokowicz. According to Mac-

Master's statements to the FBI, made eighteen years after the incident, she first takes Brokowicz home with her to Washington, D.C. But, finding herself unable to deal with the woman, she places her in a South Philadelphia hospital. There Poyntz visits her. At the sight of Poyntz, Brokowicz becomes violently agitated.

Poyntz now makes further arrangements. She obtains passports for MacMaster and Brokowicz and books passage for them on the *Normandie*, sailing for France. She also arranges for the two women to be accompanied by a Dr. Julius Littinsky and his wife, Tillie. The foursome set sail on September 2, 1936. MacMaster remains in Paris for three days, after which she leaves Brokowicz with the Littinskys and returns to the United States. She believes that the Littinskys have been instructed to win the confidence of Brokowicz and then to turn her over to people whom Poyntz has called "friends from Poland."

Questioned by the FBI in 1953, the Littinskys will reluctantly acknowledge that Poyntz had asked them to befriend the two women but, they say, they had only the most casual contact on the ship and did not see them at all after their arrival in Paris. Dr. Littinsky, who at the time was chief medical examiner for the International Workers Order and treasurer of the *Morning Freiheit*, both institutions closely associated with the Communist Party, denies that he was ever a Communist. He and his wife say that they did not know Poyntz well, although Mrs. Littinsky thinks she may have been on the pier on the day they sailed. The only purpose of their trip abroad was to celebrate their twentieth wedding anniversary, and after a stay in Paris they traveled by train through Germany and Poland and on to the Soviet Union, where they visited relatives.

Rwyka Brokowicz now disappears from our story. We may hope that she was merely an unstable woman to whom Juliet Stuart Poyntz extended a disinterested helping hand, and that once in Poland, or wherever, Brokowicz was reunited with the boy whose photograph she carried from the train. But let us remember that this is 1936, and that Juliet Poyntz is not a free agent.

If the abduction—and let us call it that—of Rwyka Brokowicz causes less than a tiny ripple in 1936, the disappearance of Juliet Poyntz nine months later was noticed by a few more people for, in certain circles, Poyntz was quite well known.

Juliet Poyntz was born in Omaha, Nebraska, in 1886 to firmly middle-class parents; her father was a lawyer, her mother was a public school teacher. Juliet, evidently a girl of exceptional abilities, was sent East to take her undergraduate degree at Barnard College. She went on to receive a master's degree at Columbia University. Early on, she was seized by an interest in immigrants and in the labor movement. In 1908, she worked for the U.S. Immigration Commission. In 1909, she joined the Socialist Party. In 1910, she was awarded a fellowship by the American Federation of Women's Clubs and went abroad to study at the London School of Economics and at Oxford University. In England she met Frederich Franz Ludwig Glaser, a German from a family of wealthy industrialists, and they married in the United States in 1913. The marriage was not a success. It seems to have lasted three or four years, on and off, and by the 1920s few of Poyntz's friends knew that she had ever had a husband, although she and Glaser remained legally married until his death in 1935.

By all accounts Poyntz was an attractive woman: medium tall, hazel-eyed, good-looking enough when young, but particularly winning by personal force and intelligence. A 1925 issue of *American Labor Who's Who* notes that she co-authored a book on labor, had been a lecturer in history at Columbia, Director of Labor Research for the Rand School, Director of Education for the International Ladies' Garment Workers Union, a lecturer for the Socialist Party, Director of the Workers' School in New York. And that, in 1924, she was a candidate for Congress on the Workers' Party ticket, at that point the name under which the Communist Party in the United States operated.

With all these many occupations, Poyntz was also spending substantial amounts of time abroad. At the end of 1921 she applied for a passport, stating that she intended to go to Holland, France, Germany, Italy, Belgium and other places, for purposes of tourism and study. Memos in the files of the Bureau of Investigation note that she was living in Berlin "in connection with Dutch Communists" and in touch with Willi Munzenberg, a leader of the German Communists. In June 1928, Poyntz applied for another passport, reporting that she had lost her earlier one; in 1929, saying that her 1928 passport had been lost, she again asked for and received a new passport. In 1932, she asked for and received another passport, this time using the name of Glaser. In this application, she stated that she had had no previous passports and had never resided outside the United States. In 1934, she applied for and received a passport in the name of Poyntz; in 1936, she used the name Glaser again, citing in her application only one previous passport, that issued in 1932 in the Glaser name.

We would not be deviating too far from known facts if we were to infer that Poyntz's missing passports were put to use by travelers who did not want their travels to the Soviet Union made known. Poyntz herself was spending significant time in the Soviet Union. In August 1931, for instance, she was advertised as a lecturer in Terre Haute, Indiana, offering "the opportunity of a lifetime to hear about the wonders of WORKERS RUSSIA by the most brilliant woman speaker in the American labor movement WHO HAS JUST SPENT A YEAR IN SOVIET RUSSIA."

Poyntz had also been in the Soviet Union in 1928 when, as a nonvoting delegate, she had attended the Sixth World Congress of the Communist International. At that time the American Communist movement was engaged in yet another of its factional struggles over leadership and, so preoccupied, American leaders only faintly understood the signs of internal struggle in the Russian party. The victor in this struggle would, of course, be Stalin, who had just recently managed the exile of his rival, Leon Trotsky, to Central Asia, and was now concerned with the removal of his chief remaining rival, Bukharin, head of the Comintern.

Poyntz was no stranger to internecine warfare. When she joined the Communist movement in 1921, her closest comrade had been Ludwig Lore, a friend of Trotsky's from his New York days, and a supporter of Trotsky even after he fell into disfavor in Moscow. When the Comintern called for an "ideological campaign" against Lore, Poyntz supported Lore. Then, in May 1925, the Central Executive Committee of the Communist Party of the United States circulated a four-page document entitled, "Statement Regarding Comrade Juliet Stuart Poyntz." It accused Poyntz of various crimes: of "opportunism," of being a "dilettante intellectual," of "not admitting the errors of her right deviations," and, more specifically, of presenting a program of education at the Workers' Party School which was incompatible with the Comintern program of education; and of selecting teachers for the school who were "nonmembers of the Party," and as such unqualified to teach subjects that she well knew "can be taught only by those who have a firm grasp of Communism." These crimes of the highest order made her "an unstable and dangerous influence. . . ." That she had already capitulated and said that she would surrender her positions in order to support the Comintern and the Central Executive Committee only showed her opportunism and condemned her "out of her own mouth." In July 1925, the *Daily Worker* called for the liquidation of "Poyntzism" as well as "Loreism."

Unlike her comrade Lore, unlike Benjamin Gitlow, James Cannon, Jay Lovestone, Bertram Wolfe and other early Party leaders who, at various times, deliberately deviated from Party policy, chose the wrong allies, or simply misread signs, Poyntz was not forced out of the party; nor did she leave for reasons of conscience. We may take it that she had been utterly sincere in saying that she would follow the policies of the Comintern and the CEC over her own inclinations; that without reservation she believed that the wind of history blew from Moscow.

The years following Poyntz's 1925 crisis find her at the public forefront of the party—running for Attorney General of New York State in 1928, and, in 1929, serving as National Secretary of the International Labor Defense, the party's most important "mass," or front, organization.

In the early months of 1934, Poyntz led a demonstration of the unemployed at New York's City Hall; at another

[*147*]

point during that winter, she spoke to a demonstrating
crowd in front of the Austrian Consulate. In the spring,
as we know, she applied once again for a passport. On
her application she wrote that she intended to leave the
country aboard the *Europa* on April 8, and to remain
abroad for six months. It is not clear exactly when she returned home, but when she did, her habits were changed.
She withdrew from all public party activities. There was
nothing dramatic about it; no statements were issued,
no differences of opinion were reported. Poyntz simply
wasn't around any more. No doubt some people wondered; others, who knew how to read the signs, assumed
that she had been recruited for what was euphemistically
known as "special work."

From late 1934 until the summer of 1936, little is known
about Poyntz's whereabouts or activities. But in November 1935 her husband, Frederich Glaser, died. For some
time Glaser had been loosely connected with the German
Consulate; his friends there were surprised to learn that
he had a wife when, in June 1936, Elias Lieberman,
Poyntz's lawyer, made a claim on behalf of his widow
for Glaser's estate.

Glaser's estate was very large, but the bulk of his wealth
remained in what by then was a Germany under Hitler's
Third Reich. Lieberman, an old friend of Poyntz's, told
her that unless she pressed her claim inside Germany,
she would realize only about twelve thousand dollars.
According to Lieberman, Poyntz replied that she would
have to consult someone before making a decision on the
matter. Lieberman asked no questions. He had known
Poyntz for almost twenty years, was very attached to her,
differed with her politically and had heard from mutual
friends that she was, at the present time, working for
Soviet intelligence.

While Lieberman began litigation for the portion of
Glaser's estate accessible to his client, Poyntz sailed for
Europe in October 1936, her passport, as we know, under
the name of Glaser. (We may recall here that this was
little more than a month after Rwyka Brokowicz set sail.)

When Poyntz returned to the United States four months
later, she instructed Lieberman not to take legal steps
to procure the German portion of Glaser's estate. Lie-

berman assumed that the decision had been made in Moscow (others would report that Poyntz had been in Moscow in 1936 and early 1937, and that she had at least once been seen there in the company of one George Mink, a known Soviet agent with a reputation for brutality. The Moscow purge trials had begun in August 1936, and during the next two years it was not only the Old Bolsheviks who suffered extermination, but also many foreign Communist agents who were called "home" to Moscow during this time, never to be heard of again. A high-ranking defecting agent, Ignatz Reiss, was assassinated in Switzerland in 1937; his replacement, Walter Krivitsky, defected soon after and was found dead in Washington under mysterious circumstances a few years later. Whittaker Chambers, receiving his summons "home" in July 1937, managed to delay and prepared to defect.

Poyntz must surely have felt trepidation when she sailed for Europe in October 1936. The situation she found in Moscow was enough to shake her faith. In May

Edward Sorel

1937, she would tell the anarcho-syndicalist Carlo Tresca that, in Moscow, her own loyalty had been questioned, but that she had allayed suspicion; and that thereafter, as a certified loyal agent, she had been assigned, with George Mink, to interrogate others.

When Poyntz returned to the United States in February 1937, still an agent of Soviet intelligence, she had seven months to figure out what she wanted to do. Only seven months, because she carried with her a return ticket showing a third-class reservation aboard the *Britannic*, due to sail from New York on September 18, 1937. She was expected back "home."

On May 14, 1937, Poyntz sent a note to Elias Lieberman: "You got away with something when last we met. So I am taking this method of getting even. You see, I hope to be able to have lunch with you some time again." The meaning of the note is obscure; perhaps there was a clarifying enclosure. But the tone seems flirtatious. Poyntz was no longer a young woman; her photographs in these later years do not show her to be particularly attractive. She was, however, a woman accustomed to having male admirers—Lieberman professed himself to be one of them—and a number of people would tell the FBI that it was "common knowledge" that a man named Schachno Epstein had been her lover, on and off, over a long period of time.

Epstein's history was outlined by Carlo Tresca in 1938, when he accused Epstein of having had a hand in Poyntz's disappearance. The two had met and become lovers more than twenty years earlier, when both had worked for the ILGWU. After the revolution in Russia, Epstein had returned to his birthplace. In the late 1920s, as an agent of the Soviet secret police, the GPU, using the name Joseph Berson, Epstein began at various intervals to visit the United States. Apparently he and Poyntz resumed their relationship. In 1933, Berson arrived in New York to edit the Yiddish-language Communist newspaper *Freiheit*. He returned to the Soviet Union sometime in 1935. He was seen in New York in the spring of 1937 by Tresca.

Toward the end of May 1937, Poyntz visited Lieberman's office and told him that she was badly in need of

Edward Sorel

money. Lieberman thought that he could get an advance of about a thousand dollars from Glaser's estate, and that he should have the money early in June. Poyntz said that she would see him then.

During the last week of May and the first days of June, Poyntz was seen in New York by a number of people. Tresca would testify that he met her by chance on the street late in May; it was then, having known him for a quarter of a century, and knowing him to be a militant anti-Stalinist, that she told him of her disillusion in Moscow. Another old friend, Sophie Theis, told the FBI that she had had lunch with Poyntz in late May, at which time Poyntz told her, in Theis's words, "I have extricated myself from my former connections and I am now going to do some writing." When she and Poyntz parted, they made a date to meet two weeks later.

On June 4, Poyntz failed to keep an appointment with her doctor. Nor did she get in touch with Lieberman to see about the money he had for her. Lieberman tried to reach her by telephone. When he could not, he was not surprised, since he was accustomed to her habits of travel. Knowing what he did about her activities he did not raise an alarm.

Poyntz had been living in a one-room apartment at the American Women's Association Clubhouse on West Fifty-seventh Street. Toward the end of June, when she had not paid her rent, an employee of the Clubhouse brought Lieberman the return portion of Poyntz's steamship ticket, which had apparently been left at the Clubhouse desk for safekeeping. Some six months passed. No one heard from Poyntz, and no one reported her missing. On December 17, 1937, a report of her disappearance appeared in several New York City newspapers. The Communist Party was asked to comment and two separate statements were prepared. Clarence Hathaway, editor of the *Daily Worker*, said: "Miss Poyntz was a member of our party for a number of years, terminating her membership toward the end of 1934. She left the party without any 'rift' but apparently to occupy herself with other interests. Since then we have not followed her activities and are quite uninformed as to her working during this past period and her interests or present whereabouts." A true enough statement as far as it went. The spokesman for the National Membership Department of the Party claimed complete ignorance: "We have no record of the woman as a member of the Communist Party and no knowledge of her whereabouts for ten years."

It is only fair to say now that exactly what happened to Poyntz remains a mystery. The closest to a sustained narrative of events was developed by Carlo Tresca and the journalist Herbert Solow. Their version was confirmed in some detail by other acquaintances of Poyntz's.

On February 8, 1938, Tresca gave a statement to United States Attorney Francis Mahony. Tresca told Mahony that due to his long friendship with Poyntz, she had confided that "she had turned from great admiration to great disgust for the way things are done in and from Russia. The Stalinites had to destroy her because she knew too much." Tresca named Schachno Epstein as a man in whom Poyntz had trust, enough trust to follow him to a place where others could take her, forcibly if necessary, to a ship bound for Russia, or perhaps even assassinate her on American soil. "The telephone operator at Juliet Poyntz's hotel told me Miss Poyntz had received a telephone call a short time before she disappeared, and that shortly after that call, a man appeared to see her. That man answers the description of [Schachno Epstein.]" Tresca testified to the same effect before a grand jury on February 21, adding that Epstein had left the country on the *Queen Mary* on August 11, 1937, using papers that identified him as Sam Stone. The FBI would later confirm that Epstein had indeed left the country in just that way.

At least two other people who knew Epstein believed that he had been involved in Poyntz's disappearance, Samuel Margoshes, of the *Jewish Daily Day*, and Simon Weber of the *Daily Forward*. Both knew of Epstein's long association with Poyntz and thought, though without evidence, that he would have been used in a kidnapping. Elias Lieberman, however, did not believe it; shortly after Tresca's charges had been made public, he received a visit from Epstein's son, Arnold. Schachno Epstein was by then in Moscow; Arnold assured Lieberman that his father was innocent and wanted Lieberman to know it.

In the midst of these events, Tresca received a letter from the American anarchist Emma Goldman in London. They had not been in touch since Goldman's deportation in 1919. "I see that you have added a new job to the many," Goldman wrote, and "that is to show up the long arm of Stalin. Well, I do not envy you! . . . They are capable of murder open and underhand as they have proven for a very considerable number of years . . ." She spoke of the danger Tresca was putting himself into, and of her own recoil from using the instruments of the capitalist system, but concluded, still, "I think you should go ahead and expose the disappearance of Miss Poyntz."

Tresca and Solow could take matters no further, however. Nor could the FBI or the Bureau of Missing Persons. Poyntz's belongings contained no clues to her whereabouts. She had taken nothing with her, not clothes, not her passport. Her trunks, which were stored in a warehouse, contained only a number of books and notebooks containing material for a projected history of modern Europe.

"Where is Juliet Stuart Poyntz?" Colonel Boris Bykov, espionage superior of Whittaker Chambers, asks his agent in 1938. Delighted with his mastery of the American idiom, he answers himself gaily: "Gone. Gone with the wind."

"My brother used to say," Nadezhda Mandelstam wrote, "that the decisive part of the subjugation of the intelligentsia was played not by terror and bribery (though, God knows, there was enough of both) but by the word 'Revolution,' which none of them could bear to give up."

HALLUCINATING THE PAST
JEWS WITHOUT MONEY REVISITED

Morris Dickstein

In everything but his lifelong loyalty to the Party, Michael Gold was the representative Communist intellectual of the twentieth century. Born Itshok Isaac Granich to an immigrant family on the Lower East Side in 1893, he Christianized his name to Irwin Granich until about 1920, when he began writing as Michael Gold, a name he borrowed from an old veteran of Lincoln's army. Unlike other American writers who flirted with Communism only at the height of the Depression, Gold came to the Party early and stayed late. He died in 1967.

Converted to radicalism when he heard a speech by the fiery Elizabeth Gurley Flynn at a Union Square rally in 1914, he bought his first copy of the *Masses*, began to contribute poems and stories, became an anarchist and got to know the whole Village bohemian world of Max Eastman, Floyd Dell, and John Reed, fled to Mexico to avoid Wilson's draft, and returned to join the Communist Party around 1920. While Gold was away, the *Masses* was closed down by the government for opposing the war; its editors were put on trial twice in 1918 for conspiring to obstruct recruitment, charges which resulted each time in a hung jury.

The defunct magazine quickly had a successor, the *Liberator*, which at first tried to revive its style of irreverent, freewheeling radicalism despite the impact of the Bolshevik triumph in the Soviet Union. Socialism now had a geographical base, even an imperfect image of the promised land, but not yet a monolithic orthodoxy. Gold became an editor of the *Liberator* in 1920 and he soon published a dithyrambic, Whitmanesque manifesto, "Towards Proletarian Art," that expressed an almost mystical affinity for the common man, the bottom dogs of society, a commitment that went deeper in him than Marxism or any other ideology.

In many ways it is a callow document, youthful, poetic, immature, eulogizing the Revolution as a form of pan-

theistic reverence for life. The text breathes an Emersonian euphoria rather than a Marxian logic. ("The Social Revolution today is not the mere political movement artists despise it as. It is Life at its fullest and noblest. It is the religion of the masses, articulate at last.") But Gold's deterministic message stood Emerson on his head, for he saw the artist as the articulate voice of the mass of men who spoke through him, the conditions that produced him. When Gold talks about the tenement world he came from, his woolly, lyrical language takes on a momentary authenticity:

> I was born in a tenement. . . . The sky above the airshafts was all my sky; and the voices of the tenement neighbors in the airshaft were the voices of all my world. . . .
> All I know of Life I learned in the tenement. I saw love there in an old mother who wept for her sons. I saw courage there in a sick worker who went to the factory every morning. I saw beauty in little children playing in the dim hallways, and despair and hope and hate incarnated in the simple figures of those who lived there with me. When I hope it is the tenement hoping, I am not an individual; I am all that the tenement group poured into me during those years of my spiritual travail.

At this stage of his life Gold, though already a Communist, was more a literary figure than the political person he would become (after 1933) as a regular *Daily Worker* columnist, the most reliable and vituperative of Stalinist hatchet men. But the Gold of 1921 was still the bohemian, a Greenwich Village original who was writing experimental plays for Eugene O'Neill's Provincetown Players. After he had suffered a nervous breakdown and left the editorship of the *Liberator* in the early twenties, he objected strongly when the magazine was turned over to the Communist Party and when he heard that one of the editors was giving up literary work to become a Party functionary.

Soon Gold was in correspondence with Upton Sinclair about starting up a new magazine that would be genuinely literary, that would print proletarian prose and dredge up inglorious Miltons from the depths of the working class. This led eventually to the creation of the *New Masses*, Gold's vehicle for proletarian experimentalism. As editor in 1930, he attacked the Party publishing house for putting out dull doctrinal works in economics rather than taking chances on the creative outpourings of the masses. At this point—the year of *Jews Without Money*, his only successful book—Gold was a proletarian writer and critic rather than a Communist Party spokesman. Our stereotyped image of him as a venomously obedient Party *apparatchik* is in need of some revision.

The later Gold was undoubtedly a nasty propagandist who swallowed every shift and betrayal, every violent twist of policy the Party sent his way. Thanks to these sharp turns, nearly all his writer friends from the teens and twenties (when he knew everyone) fell off the train of History. And Gold was there to wield a particularly brutal style of invective to castigate them all as renegades; indeed, as more writers left, apostasy became one of his chief obsessions.

With his tough-guy manner and hard-boiled, telegraphic prose, Gold could have become an American Brecht, but he lacked the German playwright's instinct for survival and his canny ironic temperament, which complicated every proletarian pose into an avant-garde gesture. In his trajectory from expressionist playwright to East German institution, Brecht held onto his West German publisher and kept his eye trained ruthlessly on his craft and his career. At some cost, he evaded the paralyzing orthodoxies that enveloped Gold and snuffed out his artistic energy.

For all his gruff, truculent demeanor—like Brecht, he kept himself rough and dirty on principle—Gold was sentimental about the tenement, sentimental about art, and sentimental about the Revolution. But only the first of these offered him a real subject, though it belonged to his distant past. Gold's first sketch toward a Lower East Side novel came out in 1917 in the *Masses*. Pieces of *Jews Without Money* appeared in magazines during the 1920s, at the height of Gold's literary career. Additional sketches, as good as anything in the book, were published as a series of ten newspaper columns as late as 1959. Gold's childhood lasted him a lifetime; the New York slums of the turn of the century became his imaginative capital, his obsession, the ground of his religious attachment to the Revolution.

On the last page of his novel, describing his sudden conversion to Communism, he addresses the Revolution as a divinity that had dispelled his dark spirits and answered to his inchoate messianic longings:

> O Workers' Revolution, you brought hope to me, a lonely, suicidal boy. You are the true Messiah. You will destroy the East Side when you come, and build there a garden for the human spirit.

Others who had grown up poor shunned even the memory of poverty and sought comfort and security. For Gold, the Revolution was his way of keeping faith with his early life, remaining true to the mother who fought boss and landlord and pawnbroker to protect her brood. "She would have stolen or killed for us," he says. "She would have let a railroad train run over her body if it could have helped us." This leads to a revealing, overwrought apostrophe: "Momma! Momma! I am still bound to you by the cords of birth. I cannot forget you. I must remain faithful to the poor because I cannot be faithless to you." The ghetto, with its dreadful miseries and deep communal loyalties, held the key to his radicalism.

Just as the Lower East Side represented everything the Revolution promised to obliterate, so its horrors justified everything done in the Revolution's name. When Trotsky was in favor, Gold wrote about him as the Leonardo of the Revolution. After his fall, Gold confessed that "I, for one, can shed no tears for him; I care for something greater than Trotsky's fate; the proletarian revolution." Telling the truth was only the first casualty of this overriding commitment. Some would say that Gold's work is fatally damaged by the ethical morass into which this blind faith led him; most of it is. But until the last page, Gold was able to keep politics and ideology out of *Jews Without Money*. He turned his recollections into grimly powerful vignettes without belaboring their message. To an unusual extent for a Communist writer, he let his material speak for itself.

Despite its sociological title, the book has the power of a series of hallucinations, especially in the opening chapters. Though *Jews Without Money* was the first of the proletarian novels of the 1930s, and one of the very few to succeed commercially—it went through eleven printings in the first nine months after publication—Gold's feverish prose set his work apart from other proletarian writers, who mimicked the bare flatness of Hemingway without the implied depths of feeling.

We can hardly avoid being prejudiced against the later Gold as an apologist for party hacks and "enlightened" murderers. But the tenement world of *Jews Without Money* imposes itself on us with the same urgency that made it dominate him. From the opening sentence—"I can never forget the East Side street where I lived as a boy"—we feel that a demon has gripped Gold by the throat and forced him to testify. In Gold's apprentice sketch for the *Masses* in 1917, this material was safely distanced and stiffly literary, as if Gold were trying to validate an undignified subject with polished writing. In *Jews Without Money*, this literary texture is stripped away like superfluous insulation.

When his memories take possession of him, Gold, like the old epic writers, becomes the vessel of his muse; he slips into the second person, addressing his characters directly as if he had raised them from the grave. One chapter begins with just such a summoning:

> Joey Cohen! You who were sacrificed under the wheels of a horse car, I see you again, Joey! I see your pale face, so sensitive despite its childish grime and bruises.

At another point, young Mikey Gold—named for Gold's pen name, not for Granich—actually *dreams* the world that surrounds him, as all the tenement families spend a stifling summer night on the roof:

> I woke one hot choking night and saw it all like a bad dream. I saw the mounds of pale stricken flesh tossing against an unreal city. I was frightened, and didn't know where I was. Then I cried, and wondered what would

MAY DAY, 1934   Edward Loul

happen if I jumped off the roof. My mother heard me, and soothed me, and I went back to sleep.

In Gold's hallucinatory vision, the immigrant families squashed together on the airless roof are like the mass of blighted humanity in the ghetto itself—"mounds of pale stricken flesh tossing against an unreal city." Gold's memories are vivid but also emblematic; they yield a half-demented poetry of human wretchedness. Only the gentle strength of the tenement mother can soothe the suicidal fears of the morbid, tormented youth.

These brutal snapshots of street and tenement life are pretty much all that happens in *Jews Without Money*, for the book is less a story than a series of dreamlike memories leading to a final awakening. We go from the whores and the street gangs to the dreadful decline of Gold's father, a gregarious storyteller and hapless businessman, who gradually succumbs to lead poisoning after years of work as a house painter. As he fades, Gold's mother emerges as the strong one, the family breadwinner, an instinctive radical who wills Gold her toughness as his father wills him his imaginative gift. But all this is less important than the social material and the atmosphere: the impassioned, exclamatory way Gold recaptures his poverty-ridden childhood.

Even if we grant, as few critics have done, that Gold created a powerful style of his own, a style sharply different from documentary naturalism or socialist realism, this doesn't explain why *Jews Without Money*, set at the turn of the century, was such a seminal text of the Depression years. Though the book was completed by the end of 1928, well before the Crash, its appearance early in 1930 helped put poverty, ethnicity, and human misery on the cultural agenda just as the Depression was putting them on the political agenda. Henry James, after his return visit to America in 1904, reported on his tour of the East Side with a fascinated horror. This teeming polyglot world was not the America he recognized, but he saw it as the face of the future. By 1930 that future had arrived, and, as Marcus Klein has argued in *Foreigners*, cultural outsiders like Gold were better equipped to write about it than the sheltered scions of New York or New England gentility. The ghetto of 1900, once barely visible to the larger culture, suddenly spoke volumes to the social distress of 1930.

Poverty was an alien subject for most middle-class authors. With the exception of possessed writers like Dickens or Hardy, those who had grown up poor preferred to forget their early struggles and humiliations. The persistence of want in the middle of prosperity is readily forgotten and continually rediscovered—by Hugo and Eugène Sue, along with Carlyle, Marx and Engels, in the mid-nineteenth century; by Zola and Gissing in the 1880s, Jack London and Upton Sinclair in the first years of the twentieth century, and, much later, by empathetic social observers like Oscar Lewis and Michael Harrington amid the affluence of the late 1950s.

The poor may always be with us, but we seem to notice them only at thirty-year intervals, like spoilers at a party for people of good conscience. The Depression was one of those moments of massive visibility, when many in the middle class were impoverished too, and proved less able to deal with it than the chronic poor. As a witness from the lower depths, Michael Gold was a forerunner of Depression writing who had nurtured angry memories and a lonely radicalism through the postwar boom. In a tribute to one of his favorite writers, Upton Sinclair, Gold found in him

> a faint trace of the Protestant minister that I can't enjoy. It is my only quarrel with this great writer. I do not relish these easy victories of virtue. There is nobility in the revolutionary camp; there is also gloom, dirt, and disorder. . . . I dislike pictures of cheerful and virtuous poverty such as Upton often draws.

Exposing the gloom, dirt, and disorder bred by poverty became Gold's specialty, his mission, "my own obsession," he called it. The stalwart workers and happy peasants of Soviet film and fiction were not his glass of tea.

As Gold was writing, the Jewish ghetto was already being burnished with nostalgia by many who had done all they could to get away from it. This process has accelerated ever since. Gold stressed the opposite, the fifty-cent-a-night whores who swallowed carbolic acid, the bed-bugs that even a Jewish mother could not eliminate. After being told by his pious mother that God made everything in the world, he wonders:

> Did God make bedbugs? One steaming hot night I couldn't sleep for the bedbugs. They have a peculiar nauseating smell of their own; it is the smell of poverty. They crawl slowly and pompously, bloated with blood, and the touch and smell of these parasites wakens every nerve to disgust.

Gold adds a rare sociological comment, in parenthesis, as if to supply his recollections with a theme, a justification:

> (Bedbugs are what people mean when they say: Poverty. There are enough pleasant superficial liars writing in America. I will write a truthful book of Poverty; I will mention bedbugs.)

A paragraph later, Gold concludes by hinting at the radical implications he will hammer home at the end of the book. His mother ("as clean as any German house-wife") repeatedly changes the sheets, sprays the mattresses, douses the beds with kerosene, but to no avail. Tinkering and reform were not enough; on her own the individual could do little to improve the conditions of the ghetto:

> The bedbugs lived and bred in the rotten walls of the tenement, with the rats, fleas, roaches; the whole rotten structure needed to be torn down; a kerosene bottle would not help.

"The whole rotten structure needed to be torn down"—not a fashionable view today, even of urban renewal, but it became one of the battle cries of the '30s. Many other episodes were parables pointing implicitly in the same direction, toward the revolutionary turn on the last page of the book, which critics have always dismissed as a *deus ex machina*. But Gold wasn't a writer who adopted revolutionary ideas when they were fashionable or abandoned them when they had gone out of fashion. The revolution was betrayed, but not for him. The pogroms of Europe were still buzzing in his ear, and new horrors were already on the horizon. The Jew as victim had merged in his mind with the proletarian as victim. His memories of the ghetto were reshaped into his hatred of capitalism. He had seen the poison of poverty make young people desperate, middle-aged people old and sick before their time, and old people grotesque and deformed. The hope of revolution had allayed the fever in his own blood.

Jews Without Money could easily be renamed, after Sherwood Anderson, "The Book of the Grotesque" (the original title of *Winesburg, Ohio*), but Gold's repulsively vivid characters are much more colorful and exotic than Anderson's small-town eccentrics. "He was a bum in moldy, wrinkled clothes saturated like a foul kitchenrag with grease," Gold says of the man who soon tries to molest little Joey Cohen. "His rusty yellow face was covered with sores. He was gruesome. He was like a corpse in the first week of decomposition." Gold's old Hebrew teacher fares no better: "The man was a walking, belching symbol of the decay of orthodox Judaism. What could such as he teach anyone? He was ignorant as a rat. He was a foul smelling, emaciated beggar who had never read anything." A newly arrived immigrant who freeloads off Gold's family, Fyfka the Miser, seems hardly distinguishable from an animal:

> He was squat, with a glum black muzzle, and nostrils like a camel. A thatch of black uncombed hair fell down his forehead, over small eyes, too bright and too morbid, like a baboon's. One arm was twisted, and he never smiled, he never said a pleasant word, he was always scratching himself, he never cleaned his nose.

These three characters aren't entirely representative: all are sadistic, ungenerous, warped in their sexuality—pure products of poverty and ignorance even in their physical deformities. A certain sameness, a badgering insistence, creeps into these portraits as if Gold, with uncontrolled disgust, were exorcising figments of his childhood as Gothic nightmare. At other moments a vein of

[*165*]

tenderness and sentiment infuses all this ugliness with
lyricism, as in Gold's apostrophe to the rare open lots that
gave children a respite from the claustral tenements:

> Shabby old ground, ripped like a battlefield by work-
> ers' picks and shovels, little garbage dump lying forgot-
> ten in the midst of tall tenements. O home of all the
> twisted junk, rusty baby carriages, lumber, bottles, boxes,
> moldy pants and dead cats of the neighborhood—every
> one spat and held the nostrils when passing you. But in
> my mind you still blaze in a halo of childish romance. No
> place will ever seem as wonderful again.

Perhaps on the basis of such passages, the few literary
critics who remember Gold attack him as a sentimentalist
and bad stylist. ("Gold was a writer whom almost any
student of literary style can criticize," wrote Allen Gutt-
mann in *The Jewish Writer in America*.) To me Gold's
work at such heightened moments takes on some Homeric
qualities he assimilated from two of his favorite writers,
Whitman and Tolstoy. From Tolstoy he learned simplicity,
directness, a preternatural clarity of outline. (He always
insisted that Tolstoy was Hemingway's true teacher.)
From Whitman he borrowed the direct Homeric apostrophe, the rolling catalogue, the tenderness toward creatures and things—like this *un*forgotten junkyard—that
become emblematic of all despised rejects who make up
the ghetto.

Despite these influences, Gold does not sound much like
any writer before or since. When I first tried reading him,
in the truncated edition Avon published soon after its
success with Henry Roth's *Call It Sleep*, I was put off by
what seemed to be a lack of texture: the staccato paragraphs, the succession of abrupt little snapshots that are
meant to feel raw and authentic—as if a prose less jagged,
more fluent, would inevitably have been less honest. ("All
these things happened," he says, after describing the pros-
titutes of Chrystie street. "They were part of our daily
lives, not lurid articles in a Sunday newspaper.")

Later I came to realize that his abrupt, impacted little
sentences and paragraphs were long-limbed lines of prose-
poetry, overheated, feverishly autobiographical, charged
with hyperbole for all their would-be realism. Gold was

the missing link between the plebeian Whitman, whom he idolized, and the youthful Allen Ginsberg, who must have read him as a Young Communist in the '30s or early '40s. Once this is noticed, it's hard to imagine the impassioned, surreal language of poems like *Howl* or "America" or "Sunflower Sutra" without thinking of certain slightly nutty passages like this one from *Jews Without Money*:

> America is so rich and fat, because it has eaten the tragedy of millions of immigrants.
>
> To understand this, you should have seen at twilight, after the day's work, one of our pick and shovel wops watering his can of beloved flowers. Brown peasant, son of thirty generations of peasants, in a sweaty undershirt by a tenement window, feeling the lost poetry. Uprooted! Lost! Betrayed!

Like Gold, Ginsberg was a Jewish visionary touched by messianic hopes, a reader of Whitman and Blake mesmerized by the American junkyard and its outcast inhabitants. As a child of the postwar era, son of a mad Communist mother, Ginsberg looked at the Revolution not as the promised redeemer but as the God that failed. To Gold's urban fierceness he added a zany humor; his was a cartoon America of supermarkets, bughouses, atom bombs, and *Time* magazine.

Gold grew up in a generation that still dreamed the American dream. But there was also the other America he knew from the tenement, the one he wanted the world to notice and change. ("My parents hated all this filth. But it was America, one had to accept it.") For him the uprooted, the lost, the betrayed were real people in a social landscape, memories that could not be put by; for Ginsberg, the postwar writer, they are figures in a personal rhetoric, a quest for spiritual self-definition. He looked to a revolution in consciousness, not a dictatorship of the proletariat.

For Gold and his family, pressed by the struggle for survival, poverty is a curse, the ghetto a trap. "The city is locked against me! I am a man in a trap!" his father groans in his demoralizing slide from businessman to house painter to street peddler, from health to illness, as he is no longer able to support his family. For Ginsberg and his Beat friends, poverty was like a set of voluntary vows, the rejection of a money culture; Gold's decrepit Lower East Side was their chosen refuge from consumerism, family life, and upward mobility.

Gold, like Ginsberg, created a style of his own, but his purpose lay beyond language; his newspaper column was called "Change the World!"; altering consciousness was a means, not an end. The contrast between him and Ginsberg measures the distance between the social radicalism of the '30s, still dreaming of an equality achieved through political upheaval, and the cultural radicalism of the '60s, adrift from the historical certitudes of Marxism, inventing its own personal legends, conjuring up more private forms of community and utopia.

KITES

W. S. Merwin

No one who did not have to
would stay in the heaving sepia
roar of the unlit depot hour
after hour as some do
shoved and elbowed in the hot
breath of a rotting mouth yet there are
women sitting on the cement floor
suckling babies and among

the shoes that are never still
down under the shouting and the thin
flickering of hands burning and
going out there are some
of all ages sleeping as they
wait to be overtaken and to
wake at their time to find themselves housed
in white boards on the bench

of the almost empty car
while outside the gray window giving
onto the cooked air of the city
they see close beside them
a new life with afternoon light
shimmering as though reflected from
water along the dusty walls and
on green weeds glittering

then already before the
walls begin to slip there are the square
pieces of color in the tan
sky skipping and soaring
those small kites with invisible strings
that will beckon as guides for
so much of the way reappearing
over the first vacant

rubble fields and the children
running with raised arms in the distance
then over the scalped hill with its
family of shadows
breathless against the sky looking up
to the spirits dancing far
above them that must feel like their own
needing it appears no

wind at all to be leaping
high above the white layer of smoke
that covers what is called the world
and to be waiting with
others above the dark trees beyond
a ringing bridge a river
too slow to be real a path along
the low bank through the shade

and they keep turning to look
down from their clearer place onto roofs
at the edge of green terraces
braided houses a man
by himself planting while the hens on
the dump smoking at the end
of a lane search among waving ghosts
of translucent plastic

all the way through the foothills
and into the mountains the kites will be
watching from their own element
as long as the light lasts
neither living as the living know
of it nor dead with the dead
and neither leaving nor promising
the hands that hope for them

CONTRIBUTORS

RICK ROFIHE's stories have appeared in *Grand Street* and the *New Yorker*. His collection, *Sixteen Quarters*, will be published by Farrar, Straus & Giroux . . . SAMUEL BECKETT was born in Foxrock, a suburb of Dublin, on April 13, 1906, a Good Friday, and died in Paris on the Friday before last Christmas. His most recent books are *Stirring Still* and *Nowhow On: Company, Ill Seen and Ill Said, Worstward Ho* . . . JOAN LONDON lives in Fremantle, Western Australia. Her collection of short stories, *Sister Ships*, was published by Viking in 1987 . . . SUZANNE GARDINIER is at work on a booklength poem called "The New World" from which "Usahn" is an excerpt . . . *Woodpecker Point and Other Stories* by CARMEL BIRD was published by New Directions in 1988 . . . RICHARD HOWARD's ninth book of poems, *No Traveller*, was published by Knopf in 1989 . . . MARY GORDON's latest book is *The Other Side* (Viking) . . . ELEANOR ROSS TAYLOR's most recent book is *New and Selected Poems* (Stuart Wright) . . . THOMAS M. DISCH is the author of *Amnesia*, a computer-interactive novel (Electronic Arts) . . . KATHA POLLITT's most recent book is *Antarctic Traveller* (Knopf) . . . PHILIP MANSEL is a historian of the courts and monarchs. His latest book is *Sultans in Splendor: Monarchs of the Middle East, 1864–1945* (Vendome Press) . . . ALFRED CORN's most recent book of poems is *The West Door* (Viking). He is editor of *Incarnation: Contemporary Writers on the New Testament*, due this spring from Viking; his novel, *Part of His Story*, will appear later in the year . . . MARK STRAND teaches at the University of Utah . . . ARTHUR C. DANTO is Johnsonian Professor of Philosophy at Columbia University and art critic for the *Nation* . . . ASKOLD MELNYCZUK has stories, poems and essays in the *Antioch Review, Partisan Review, Gettysburg Review, Pequod* and elsewhere. He is the editor of *Agni* . . . AGHA SHAHID ALI is professor of English at Hamilton College and author of *The Half-Inch Himalayas*, a book of poems from Wesleyan University Press. He has completed a book of Faiz translations . . . FAIZ AHMED FAIZ was born in Punjab in 1911 and died in 1984 in Lahore . . . *All The Right Enemies: The Life and Murder of Carlos Tresca* by DOROTHY GALLAGHER was recently published in paperback by Viking/Penguin . . . MORRIS DICKSTEIN teaches English at Queens College and is the author of *Gates of Eden* (Penguin). He is currently a fellow at the National Humanities Center and is completing a book on the 1930s, from which this essay is adapted . . . W. S. MERWIN's recent books include *The Rain in the Trees* (Knopf), *Selected Poems* (Atheneum) and *Vertical Poetry* (North Point Press), translations from the poetry of Roberto Juarroz.

STATEMENT OF OWNERSHIP

Statement of Ownership, Management and Circulation (Act of August 12, 1970: Section 3685. Title 39. United States Code). No. 1. Title of publication: Grand Street. No. 2. Date of filing: 9/29/88. No. 3. Frequency of issue: quarterly. No. 4. Location of the known office of publication: 50 Riverside Drive, New York, New York 10024. No. 5. Location of the headquarters or general business offices of the publishers: 50 Riverside Drive, New York, New York 10024. No. 6. Names and addresses of publisher and editor: Deborah Thomas, publisher; Ben Sonnenberg, editor, all at 50 Riverside Drive, New York, New York 10024. No. 7. Owner: Grand Street Publications, Inc., Ben Sonnenberg, 50 Riverside Drive, New York, New York 10024. No. 8. Known bondholders, mortgagees, and other security holders owning or holding 1 percent or more of the total amount of bonds, mortgages, or other securities: none. No. 9. For optional completion by publishers mailing at regular rates. No. 10. Extent and nature of circulation. Average number of copies each issue during preceding 12 months. No. A. Total number of copies printed 4,000. No. B. Paid circulation: 1. Sales through dealers and carriers, street vendors, and counter sales: 1,825. 2. Mail subscriptions: 1,600. No. C. Total paid circulation: 3,425. No. D. Free distribution by mail, carrier, or other means; samples, complimentary and other free copies: 230. No. E. Total distribution: 3,655. No. F. Copies not distributed: 1. Office use, left over, unaccounted, spoiled after printing: 145. 2. Return from news agents: 200. No. G. Total: 4000. Actual number of copies of single issue published nearest to filing date. No. 11. I certify that the statements made by me above are correct and complete. Signature of editor or publisher: Deborah Thomas, publisher.

STORY QUARTERLY 26

Single Issue $4/4 Issues $12
P.O. Box 1416, Northbrook, IL 60065